HEARTPATHS
FOR HARD TIMES

Praise for *HeartPaths for Hard Times*

Excellent! A book I will share with many people. . . . powerful true stories of hope and healing.

— **Alie Palmer**
Retired nurse and Shaklee Lifetime Coordinator

Stories of overcomers have the power to rekindle the spirit. Stories and tools and the understanding to return from heartbreak or grief. No matter where you are in life, you will find this book an inspiration.

— **Rick Seymour**
Entrepreneur and Shaklee Master Coordinator

Rhoda Searcy brings an inspirational voice to heart-rending accounts of true stories about loss, grief, illness, and life transitions. Creative usable strategies for effective coping.

— **Linda LeVoy Jackson, MA Ed.**
Licensed Professional Counselor
Certified Group Psychotherapist

Rhoda's unique life experiences have fostered deep compassion and sensitivity to those whose hearts have known. . . loss and change. As nurse, teacher, and wellness entrepreneur, she leads others to discover a pathway for wholeness.

— **Dr. William H. Adams, Jr.**
Former Chair, Continuing Education,
Davidson County Community College
(North Carolina)

Life-affirming resources involving God are clearly presented as part of maintaining the courage to confront crisis, stress and trauma. Excellent for peer counseling or lay ministers.

— **Pamela O. Werstlein, Ph.D., APRN**
Family Nurse Practitioner and
Licensed Practicing Counselor

To Ellie,
Blessings and
Comfort on Your
Heart Path &
Journey Through To
Healing,
Rhoda

HEARTPATHS FOR HARD TIMES

Bridges for Coping
with Loss and Change

Rhoda Moyer Searcy, RN, MN
Rhoda Moyer Searcy, RN, MN

1025 Deepwood Ct.
Winston Salem, NC
27104

Foreword by Robert G. Allen

H♥MANOMICS
PUBLISHING

Systems where People Matter

A Grace Associates Book

Library of Congress Catalog Card Number: 2002115895

ISBN: 0-9666085-5-0

First Edition, First Printing
Printed in Canada

Cover Art: Stephen W. Dunn
Cover Design: Bruce Gore
Editorial Coordination: John Patrick Grace and Jennifer Adkins
    Grace Associates
    945 4th Avenue, Suite 200A
    Huntington, West Virginia 25701
Interior Design: Mark Phillips / Marketing+Design Group

Discounts available for bulk purchase for churches, hospitals,
schools and other organizations. Premium and Specialty printing
runs available. Please address inquiries to the publisher.

P.O. Box 2395
Huntington, West Virginia 25724
Tel. 304-697-3236 — Fax 304-697-3399
publish@cloh.net

www.booksbygrace.com

FOREWORD

Though I've become known for helping people generate monetary wealth, there are other kinds of wealth that are supremely important.

How about faith, family, and friends?

Rhoda Searcy, RN, MN, a mental health nurse with a master's degree and a dedicated protégé in my mentoring program, offers the world a treasure of wonderful stories and strategies for getting through life's toughest trials.

Virtually everything she holds up as encouragement or inspiration is anchored in either faith, family, friends—or all three.

She writes with sensitivity of a family's loss of fourteen-year-old Taylor, a boy of charm and energy, to the freak accident of an overturned tractor upon which he had been riding. And she shows how the tragic loss of Taylor brings the family closer together in their grief.

In another story, the Nichols brothers see their North Carolina tobacco farm disappear along with a vanishing market for small tobacco holdings. The brothers, full of integrity and grit, refuse to file bankruptcy and fight hard to regain solvency through a new, and unrelated, venture.

A twelve-year-old girl becomes stronger and moves toward adult responsibilities in yet another tale as the girl helps her mother cope with the degenerative disease of Lupus.

Herself a survivor of multiple crises, sometimes bunched closely together, Rhoda Searcy has developed herself as an authentic expert in counseling others on how to cope with grief, loss, and change. The integration of knowledge and experience from diverse disciplines makes this an essential handbook for anyone facing loss and change regardless of the cause or type. Practical suggestions provide a path to positive coping, adjusting paradigms and attitudes, and developing adequate support systems, all keys to personal growth and positive outcomes.

Her faith in a loving and ever-present God, nurtured during her Mennonite upbringing, resonates throughout the book.

You will also be buoyed up by the book's stirring assortment of quotes from scripture and from poets, writers and other social thinkers, of yesterday and today.

I appreciate Rhoda Searcy for the patient, deeply caring woman of faith that she is. You'll soon discover why as you journey across the inspiring landscape of *HeartPaths for Hard Times*.

— **Robert G Allen**, Author
New York Times bestselling *Nothing Down*,
Creating Wealth, Multiple Streams of Income,
Multiple Streams of Internet Income, and *The One-Minute Millionaire* (with Mark Victor Hansen)

TABLE OF CONTENTS

INTRODUCTION

Many of you drawn to this book have been shaken by painful losses of home, of work, of loved ones. You may have lost a spouse, child or close friend to death or to the "death"of alcoholism, divorce, Alzheimers, prison or some other unwanted reality. You may have experienced losses that are difficult to define, such as a "failure," role changes, or self-image changes. Your loss may be invisible to others, or socially unrecognized. I want you to know right from the start that I can empathize deeply with the grief and disorientation you have experienced.

After a heroic two-year struggle with cancer, my beloved husband Roy died at home on Christmas Eve. Our minister, one of Roy's closest friends, sat with me at his bedside as Roy entered into a new life with God.

During Roy's illness, the Dean of the graduate nursing program where I was employed had called me in and informed me that at the end of that current school year my job would end. They had lost three grants, soft money that had paid my salary. I had no time or energy to integrate my loss. This job loss was compounded by the fact that I had given up my training business, my chosen career path, when Roy was first diagnosed with cancer so we could spend more time together.

Looking back over the past few years I could count other personal and professional challenges, adding up to a total stress score that I knew was off the charts: One of my close friends had died of stomach cancer at age forty-three. Another friend and mentor in the training field had succumbed to leukemia at age fifty. Both had fought valiant battles and I had walked with them faithfully on the final stretches of their journeys through this life. What was more I myself had entered into menopause with intense night sweats that left me sleep deprived for many months. My whole life seemed to exist on shifting sand. The book you now hold, however, had been taking shape even before the streak of crises I've just cited. It began, actually, as a three-hour seminar on how people could grow emotionally and spiritually from loss and change, which mostly come upon us unbidden and unwelcomed. The seminar aimed at meeting the needs of a Fortune 500 company that had laid off thousands of people in recent years. Morale among the surviving employees was quite low, and it was for them that I developed my workshop.

Never before had I done anything like this: a training seminar dealing with intense emotional reactions to multiple traumatic losses that threatened to immobilize an entire Fortune 500 company. The budget was small, the number of participants huge. Thousands of people needed to take part over a period of six to eight weeks.

I presented a simple yet powerful package to seven trainers and taught them how to implement the design of a seminar called "Choosing to Grow from Change." They in turn made presentations to thousands of their fellow employees, with life-changing results. Emotional healing and renewed ability to focus on helping the company move ahead resulted from the process.

After altering some parts to protect my client's identity, I began to put on the seminar with other groups, corporations, small businesses, and nonprofit organizations. Every time I led the program I received positive feedback about the profound impact it had had upon participants. And so I decided I should do a book with the concepts in it as a gift to people everywhere going through major life changes, especially when due to a heart-rending loss.

The book begins with a large selection of stories, all true, of individuals and families going through loss and change. Why stories? Because stories have power to teach, to train, to inspire, to encourage and to heal the human heart. They can also change minds, habits and perceptions, and act as a bridge from where we are at the moment to where we want to go.

Sometimes when we are too close to a situation, especially a painful one, a good story can stimulate our imagination and transcend our personal history. In other words, stories can help get us unstuck from our grief or our immobility, and get back to faith and to positive action.

Next the book moves into a section called "Strategies." Here I will unfold the principles of coping I developed for the Fortune 500 company workshop and also blend in examples from my own and others' experiences of "moving through the pain" and getting restabilized.

Finally, the book includes an ample Resource section. One book or audio or videotape is rarely enough to meet all the needs of a grieving human being. It is a pleasure for me to share with you a wealth of wisdom from so many authors, speakers and organizations who have helped thousands of people navigate the shoals of life's most difficult moments.

My personal story of coping with a decade of loss and change is long and involved. Together, my publisher and I made the tough decision to focus this book on sharing many varied short stories, rather than include my lengthy one so we could keep this book at its current length. Perhaps my full story will be birthed in a future *HeartPath* volume.

I sincerely want these stories, strategies and resources to make a difference for you. It is my hope and prayer that you will find, within these pages, comfort, renewed hope, courage, and inspiration to grow your own heart path through loss and change.

— **Rhoda Moyer Searcy**, RN, MN
Winston-Salem, North Carolina
September 25, 2002

ACKNOWLEDGEMENTS

I wish to express my heartfelt gratitude to all the people who have supported and encouraged me in my journey to complete this book. The following are named with deep appreciation without assigning priority or rank:

My life mentors, including Mr. Pollack, Bishop Richard Detweiler, Pearl Schrack, Dr. Vida S. Huber, Andy White, Dr. Eloise Lewis, Dr. Josephine Lewis, Dr. Genevieve Bartol, Dr. Hazel Brown, Paul Meyer, Dr. Denis Waitley, Ron Willingham, David McNally, Bob Proctor, Bob Allen, Doug Wead, Denise Michaels, Judy Key, JoAnn Dunn, Don and Marlene Hoirup, Ann Westergaard, Beverly Willingham, Rick Seymour, Bob Fergueson, Dr. Robert H. Schuller, Dr. M. Josephine Snider, Dr. Vann Joines, Mark Meyerdirk, and Mark Victor Hanson.

My parents, David Edwin and Sarah Moyer, who gave me life, love, faith, values, and a yearning for beauty; my siblings Beula Peele, Dave Moyer, Ruth Kauffman, and Daniel Moyer who have taught me much about life; my friends who have been loyal and caring cheerleaders in spite of my long seclusion to achieve this goal, especially Diane Nations, Donna Hayden Keene, Nancy Merschat, Betty Jo Lambe (who kept an extra hard copy of drafts for me), Ken Burkel, Raine Remsburg, Justus Harris, and Elwood and Mary Walker; my step daughters, Robin Bradley and Courtney Thompson who share their lives with me.

To those friends, relatives, and professional collegues who were willing to share their stories with me for this book, Thank You! Some of your stories bear your name, others have been disguised to protect innocent parties. I am sorry a few were deleted to maintain book size. I deeply appreciate your significant contributions and your trust. Also, thanks to those friends who through the years have shared with me inspirational stories of hope and faith and goodness in the world. Some of the stories included were impossible to trace authorship, which I deeply regret and acknowledge.

To my skilled and faithful typist, Mary Barnhardt, and Laura Nations who filled in while Mary was on a mission trip to Bolivia, I am most appreciative.

I am also deeply grateful:

To my publisher and editor, Dr. John Patrick Grace, who saw the potential in my book proposal and guided this book from conception through creation and birth, persisting in spite of obstacles. To Jennifer, Mark, Bill and Amanda for their skill and assistance in mission accomplished.

To my Shaklee EDEN colleaques, especially Beverly Willingham, Ann Barry, and Shirley Koritnik who offered the gift of relief from communication responsibilities while completing this book; and my Shaklee friends Cathy Powell, Kay Goode, and Peggy Tucker who caringly encouraged me in this endeavor.

To Linda Jackson and Dr. Pamela Werstlein, faithful long term friends, whose reading and professional suggestions improved content and structure, plus encouragement as to the value of HeartPaths for clients buoyed me onward; my high school friend Freida Myers who invited me to speak at my class reunion on Change the year before my Mom died; Amie Hampton for her continuing belief in me and my ability to contribute to other's lives, who also introduced me to my cover artist, Steven Dunn. Steven, you are a treasure.

To my PWWS friends and fellow board members who warmly encouraged and supported my professional creativity. Thanks, though not wishing to leave someone out, to Judi Wallace, Kristie Staton, Amy Orser (who shared her children's book on grief so generously), Cathy Seaver, Patti Fisher, Jeanie Saphar (who stored my back up copy on her computer for safety), Phyllis Moore, Rena Waring, Theresa Gibson, Hilary Kosloske, Carann Graham, Joan Malcolm, and Amy Gardner.

I acknowledge my indebtedness to those who took time out of busy schedules to review portions of the stories and strategies: Dr. Vann Joines, Dr. Bill Adams, Rick Seymour, Alie Palmer, Dr. Robert Nations, Linda Jackson, and Dr. Pamela Werstlein.

Christopher Hayden's artistic creativity and giftedness in graphics is acknowledged along with my cover designer Bruce Gore. Together they, along with Steven W. Dunn, landscape artist, contributed greatly to the visual emotional message and artistic beauty desired for the cover. This was so important to me.

Last and not least, I am deeply grateful to the memory of my late husband, Roy Allen Searcy, a Champion with Heart, who believed I could do anything I set my mind to do, and to God Who gave me my talents and gifts and called me to make a difference with my life.

NOTE: Energetic efforts were made to identify the sources of stories in the first section of this book listed as "author unknown." The authors of these stories are heartily invited to make themselves known so that appropriate credit may be given. RMS

*Dedicated to all who have walked
the Paths of Pain or Darkness.
May you mount on eagle's wings
and soar toward Light, Hope, and Joy.*

PART ONE

STORIES

*In times of change the learners will inherit
the earth, while the learned find themselves
beautifully equipped to deal with a world
that no longer exists.*

— Eric Hoffer

1. Bridging Life's Changes and Challenges
A story from Rhoda's life

In my thirties, after a very stressful year in graduate school—when I confronted a culture at a large public university as foreign to my lifestyle and experiences as any faraway land or people—I had a dream that haunted me. It was scary and vivid, and hovered in my consciousness for months. I could not forget it.

In Atlanta, I attended a workshop by a Dr. Jack Johnston who had studied and done extensive research on the Senoia tribe of Malaysia, where there was no mental illness. Out of his studies and experiences with these tribes, he created a process for interpreting dreams. (Bringing the "night" into the light of day so that the night dreams could be integrated into one's waking hours and living.) The Senoia people always shared their dreams and discussed their symbols and meaning within the family or community each morning as they ate together.

Dr. Johnston explained his process and then asked for a volunteer to share a recurring "nightmare" so he could help apply the process as a demonstration to participants. (Most of us were therapists, or becoming therapists.) I listened carefully and saw how the woman experienced insight and relief, and then after the workshop was over, I drove home to North Carolina (over six hours). Along the drive, I kept thinking of my own scary dream. On impulse, I decided to stop at a rest stop. Seated in my car, I pulled out the written steps Dr. Johnston had given us in the workshop. I put myself in a trance and recalled the scary dream and then interpreted it by following his steps. With shock and surprise, I observed the monster animal take off its mask and become my mother. I asked her for a gift, which represented the essence of her power and presence and spirit in my life.

The image which appeared to my mind's eye was of a bridge spanning over a fast-flowing mountain stream. It seemed familiar—like I had sometime seen a bridge like that in my waking life, possibly in the Appalachian Mountains of North Carolina. It was a curved, wooden bridge: strong, sturdy, stable, simple. A path led to it and continued into woods on the other side of the rushing stream. Initially, I wanted to reject the bridge image, and ask for another one to represent my mother's spirit and power and essence. But in my trance, I decided to accept her offered gift. And then—in the Dream State—I saw myself standing on the bridge, and I threw "stuff" into the water and it turned the water very murky.

As I watched, the water cleared as it carried away the junk and garbage of the stuff thrown into it, and again became sparkling, crystal clear, and pure.

I honored and thanked the spirit of my mother and then returned to a waking, alert state, feeling free and deeply touched by the experience. Now I understood the meaning: the bridge was a great symbol for my mother and her simple way of life. My mother, who did not want me to change, had given me a priceless gift: I could throw away the things which no longer served my life, and allow new things to enter my life to serve me and help me achieve wholeness or completeness or fulfillment.

After I arrived home, the power of the experience was still with me. I drew a bridge over water with dark, murky "stuff" on one side and pure, clean water on the other side. I posted it on my kitchen cabinet and kept it there until I moved to a new home. (Dr. Johnston recommended creating a visible picture of the "gift" to help integrate it into one's life.)

Sometime later I started a new business, a personal

development and training company. When I was asked what I would call my company, I hesitated momentarily and then spoke with assurance: Bridge Enterprises. The name stood for helping people make changes in their lives from where they were to where they wanted to be. It also stood for my own "TO BE" all I could and become. I had an artist do a rendition of my vision, and she gave me several options. I chose the one that was simple, graceful, and a more modern view of my small wooden bridge on a mountain trail.

That dream became a stepping stone and a space for healing and permission to discard worn out, no longer useful practices, beliefs, attitudes so that I could replace them with those that were new, useful, and beneficial to my current life. The image of my mother symbolized my past, but she also became an internal permissive higher self who helped me bridge my childhood past with the emerging business woman who longed to make a difference in the world. I had no model for what and who I was becoming, and I needed my real mother's blessing. So my dream became that change agent and allowed my inner self to feel safe to change. It was a powerful example of how—by carefully applying techniques—one can create self-healing. Following that experience my perceptions of change became more positive and powerful, and I was able to take a leap of faith to start my own business, with no financial support from family or even from friends.

★　★　★　★　★　★　★

Everyone needs a bridge or a series of bridges to help him move from one time in life to a different stage or place. Bridges may be support people, or events that change perceptions, or activities or ideas that span the old and the new or becoming part. A bridge must be strong enough to support and carry one to the next place on life's journey. To me, bridges are transitional in nature—carrying one forward, helping to transform and change. Perhaps to span a deep gully or impassible roadway or even go through or under a mountain or river—a barrier of some kind that can hinder or stop one's momentum or progress.

For I know the thoughts that I think toward you, says the Lord. . . thoughts of peace and not evil, to give you a future and a hope. . . .

— Jeremiah 29:11

NOTE: Scriptures quoted in this book are from The New King James Version of the Bible.

Beauty of a Woman
From an email by Patti Fisher

The beauty of a woman is not in the clothes she wears,
The figure she carries, or the way she combs her hair.
The beauty of a woman must be seen from her eyes,
Because that is the doorway to her heart,
The place where love resides.
The beauty of a woman is not in a facial mole,
But true beauty in a woman is reflected in her soul.
It is the caring that she lovingly gives,
The passion that she shows.
The beauty of a woman
With passing years — only grows.

2. Gratitude Changes a Vietnam Vet's Life
A story from a friend of RMS

Richard, my husband, never talked a lot about his time in Viet Nam other than how he'd been shot by a sniper. However, he had a rather grainy, 8 x 10 black and white photo he had taken at a USO show of Ann Margaret with Bob Hope in the background. The photo was one of his treasures. A few years ago, Ann Margaret was doing a book signing at a local bookstore. Richard wanted to see if he could get her to sign the treasured photo, so he arrived at the bookstore at 12 o'clock for the 7:30 p.m. signing.

When I joined him there after work, the line went all the way around the bookstore, circled the parking lot, and disappeared behind a parking garage. Before her appearance, bookstore employees announced that Ann Margaret would sign only her book and no memorabilia would be permitted. Richard was disappointed, but still wanted to show her the photo and let her know how much those shows meant to lonely GIs far from home.

Ann Margaret came out looking as beautiful as ever and, as he was second in line, it was soon Richard's turn. He presented her the book for a signature and then took out the photo. When he did, there were protests from the employees that she would not sign it. Richard said, "I understand. I just wanted her to see it." She took one look at the photo, tears welled up in her eyes, and she said, "This is one of my gentlemen from Viet Nam and I most certainly will sign his photo. I know what these men did for our country and I always have time for 'my gentlemen.'" With that, she pulled Richard across the table and planted a big kiss on him. She then made quite a do about the bravery of the young men she had met over the years, how much she admired them, and how much she appreciated them. There weren't many dry eyes among those close enough to hear. She then posed for pictures and acted as if my husband was the only one in the place.

Later at dinner, Richard was very quiet. When I asked if he'd like to talk about it, my big strong husband broke down in tears. "That's the first time anyone ever thanked me for my time in the Army," he said. Richard, like many others, came home to people who spit on him and shouted ugly things at him.

That night was a turning point for him. He walked a little straighter and, for the first time in years, was proud to be a Vietnam Vet. I'll never forget Ann Margaret for her graciousness and how much that small act of kindness meant to my husband.

I now make it a point to say "Thank You!" to every person I come across who has served in our Armed Forces.

Freedom does not come cheap, and I am grateful for all those men and women who have made a commitment to help keep our country strong and free.

3. Accidental Death of a Teenager and Only Son/Brother
From an interview with Emilie Barnhardt, a friend of RMS

Two days after Christmas, the house was upside down after the seven-person family celebrations and everyone home from school for the holidays. Emilie had planned to straighten everything up, but three of her four daughters wanted to learn to sew. So she obliged, putting aside her desire to re-create a sense of order; she got out all the fabrics, patterns, and other materials for sewing projects. Though disorder reigned in the house she shared with her husband Roland, a minister, and their five children, the mood was one of joyful pleasure and family comraderie and fun. Internally, there was a sense of peaceful order in spite of the outer chaos. Her only son, Taylor, had gone to visit his uncle's family a couple hours' drive away.

As Emilie sat at the sewing machine, the phone rang. She answered and heard the words, "Taylor's been hurt and it's bad!" Immediately, as if responding to an unseen prompting, she prayed, "Dear God, if Taylor can't be whole, alive, and happy, You take care of him for me."

Before she could prepare to leave, the phone rang again: it was her brother with the awful truth: "I'm so sorry. Taylor is dead!"

In her heart-wrenching pain and shock of the moment, Emilie screamed from where she was in the basement to her daughters, who were two floors above: "Taylor's dead!" (It felt like an eternity, though it was only a few seconds, until she reached them two floors away from where she had been when the call came. To this day, she regrets screaming — because it jolted her daughters.) Everyone was in shock, trying to comprehend the awful truth. After Emilie screamed, however, a sense of peace enveloped her.

So she calmly spoke: "We're going to my brother's house. We need to pray for them for strength to get through this." A sense of calm, peace, and being in control came over her. She felt that God was giving her peace and the ability to focus on the needs of others. The family drove the distance to her brother's house. During the whole trip she prayed to herself and aloud, "Lord, please don't let us blame anyone or say anything that will make their pain any greater." At their house, the emergency medical vehicle was leaving. She knew it carried the body of her son.

In their house, she learned several things: the newspaper had sent a reporter who knew the family and he had told his boss he could not do the story, because of his emotional ties to the family. He was unable to cope and respond professionally, and declined to write up the event. Therefore, there were no TV and other newspaper personnel present at the site where a tractor had overturned and killed Taylor instantly. Emilie adamantly declares that people have a right as human beings to have privacy without cameras catching family in moments of grief and shock or a microphone placed in front of people's faces and questions asked. She saw her nephew, observed his grey color, and realized he had been a witness to the horror when her son — and his favorite cousin — had died. They had been trying to pull out a Bobcat which was stuck, and as the tractor, on which Taylor was seated, began to flip over, her nephew had yelled: "Jump!" But Taylor didn't jump — and so the nephew had to witness his death, as he was pinned under the tractor. It had taken several hours to get the tractor off of Taylor, so that is why the emergency vehicle was just leaving as they arrived. One of her brothers had urged the emergency people to get Taylor out before his mother arrived.

Emilie asked everyone, "Where did they take Taylor?" No one knew. Finally she learned they had taken him to the city morgue. So Emilie, Roland, her husband, and Emilie's dad went there. Emilie describes it as a "cold, hard experience."

As they entered the morgue, Emilie remembers the place being cold and quiet. There was only one man working. When Emilie asked if she could see Taylor, the kind man told her, "You have the right to see your son. However, the way he looks now is not the picture you want to remember." And so, she made the decision not to look at him at that time. She believes it was a wise decision. She asked for his things, but the attendant said they were not allowed to give them to her then.

Before the family drove to her brother's home, Emilie had contacted a close neighbor and asked if she would come into her house while the family was away and clear a path so people could walk. She told her just to put things in drawers, closets, under beds, anywhere she could find room — just tuck things away. And so, the neighbor and her daughter had come in and made everything neat, knowing they would have guests coming to visit and offer comfort. When they arrived back home, the house was crowded with people — who stayed until midnight to be with them, to offer comfort and support. At one point, as the night grew late, Emilie realized she had not had a moment to herself all day. Suddenly she felt she needed a space for quiet reflection. She went outside in the darkness and sat on the porch to steal a few minutes alone. Different times over the following days she wished for solitude. But it was hard to find. She said that, amazingly, she was able to sleep — and she felt this was a gift from God. However, for a long time, her sleep contained nightmares, in which she dreamed of the accident that took Taylor's life.

Her oldest daughter was on a trip with the high school chorus in New York. Upon arriving at the hotel, she called her parents to tell them she had arrived safely in New York. When she called home, her uncle, her father's brother, took the call. He didn't want to give her the news when she was alone. However, she sensed from his tone that something was wrong, and was afraid something had happened to one of her parents — that they had been injured or killed — so she insisted on knowing the truth. He told her to go find her group leader. She still insisted, so he said her brother had died in an accident and her parents were at her uncle's house. In her grief, she screamed and began sobbing in the hotel lobby. No one came to comfort her; finally she found her way to the group leader.

During this time, while in the New York hotel lobby, hearing this shocking, shattering news for a young southern-raised teenager all alone, she felt so terribly isolated. The sounds and sights of people in the lobby, who spoke foreign languages and represented the cultures of the world, made her feel like she was literally in another country — a foreigner in her own native land. (In acute crisis, the mind often copes by focusing on bits and pieces of the environment or situation, as a way of allowing painful truth to gradually be absorbed.)

Christin's uncle tried to get her a commercial flight home that night, but was unable to book her a seat. The family did not realize until later that they could have asked the airlines for a priority seat due to the death. However, her uncle took matters into his own hands and a friend of his took him to New York City in a small plane and together they brought Christin back to her home that night. Christin said the flight home was actually a gift because she had time to think, and feel and be angry, and process the situation for herself before she reached the house crowded with people and had to deal with others' reactions.

While flying back home, the small plane would "jump," and she had the perceptions, sensations, and memories of how Taylor would come up behind her and grab her and say "I gotcha!" So she thought about Taylor flying with them and every time the plane "jumped" she felt Taylor was saying to her: "I gotcha, Christin, I gotcha!"

On Sunday afternoon the family went to the funeral home to visit Taylor's body. Someone had suggested that the children might like something tangible to hold, so Emilie asked the girls if they wanted to choose something of Taylor's to take with them. One sister took his drumsticks, another took his basketball, and another took his cross necklace that he always wore. Emilie used his baseball cap to hide some of the trauma on the right side of his face. They made the decision to have a closed casket; that way his friends could remember him as he was when alive. Only immediate family could choose to see him, if they wanted to, and they decided to have friends visit at their home instead of at the funeral home.

The girls took the basketball, the drumsticks, and Taylor's cross necklace back home with them. Sarah played with the basketball as they left the funeral home, bouncing it up and down! Days later, the girls played with his basketball, bouncing and bouncing it on their drive, releasing emotion and anger in a healthy manner. (They continue to play with Taylor's basketball.) The cross he wore for the Christmas Eve service was given by their church to his mother to keep (which she keeps hanging in her bedroom in memory), and one like it was buried with him. Roland had special gold cross necklaces made with a star in the center, and gave them to the girls and Emilie on the six-month anniversary of Taylor's death.

We do not know what God's purposes are, but Emilie firmly believes that God can bring good out of tragedy. One of those "good" things was that Taylor's death got Emilie's family back together. For fifteen years there had been some alienation within the family, making Christmas difficult for years. That Christmas, Taylor had asked, "Will our family ever get together?" Emilie says, "In his death, Taylor got our family together." Emilie decided she wanted to "Live life fully" in memory of her son. One of her ways of coping was to write letters and to give them out to family members and close friends.

Close friends from the city in which they had previously lived and where Roland had served as pastor to a church, came and stayed at their home over the weekend and took care of them as a family. It helped in that critical period of shock and anguish going from a family of seven to a family of six.

On Sunday afternoon, they planned the service as a candlelight service for Monday and three days after Taylor's death.

Emilie was appalled at the expense and felt so vulnerable and taken advantage of when they went to make funeral arrangements for their son. She had no idea how expensive everything was.

On Sunday morning, they wanted to be back in church where they had been together as a family on Christmas Eve. Taylor had read the scripture for the youth program and candlelight service. He had read: "Do not be afraid. I bring you good news of great joy that will be for all people. Today in the town of David a Savior has been born to you; He is Christ the Lord."

After the Christmas Eve service, his parents had found Taylor putting out the candles in the sanctuary. In his memory and in celebration of his life, the family decided to relight the candles at his memorial service. And so they did: parents and four sisters lit their candles at the altar at the close of the memorial service and then began to light the almost five hundred attendees' candles until the whole church was ablaze in light. Emilie said she felt deep peace as she walked back to the front — aglow in the light — singing, "Go tell it on the mountain...that Jesus Christ is born!"

A bit of humor and insight into Taylor's approach to life and entrepreneurial potential was contained in his wallet when he died. His wallet contained four five-dollar bills. Emilie had received her first Christmas gift bought by Taylor that Christmas: a snow globe, which she still treasures. However, Taylor had paid $19.95 for the globe and had asked his sisters to contribute to the gift. The four five-dollar bills were his four sisters' "portion" of the gift!

The family has changed as a result of the tragedy. Financially conservative in the past, they became freer to spend some money to create joy. They invested money in creating a special memorial card using Taylor's art. Emilie and Roland became very intentional about not making Taylor their perfect child. They found tangible ways to honor Taylor's memory. The family made and gave away hundreds of three-dimensional stars. Taylor had taught them how to fold paper to make these stars. Emilie found great comfort by wearing Taylor's clothes. Initially, each of Taylor's sisters responded differently. Mary, eighteen months younger and very close to Taylor, who was his shadow in life, focused completely on academics and achieving high grades. Sarah, with a personality similar to Taylor's, wanted his bed to sleep in. In the sixth grade, Sarah's teacher called Emilie after Sarah wrote a story: "The Worst Phone Call Ever" for her class. The teacher did not know what to do. Consequently, Sarah was permitted and encouraged to write poems and stories that year related to her brother that helped her express her grief and heal her heart and spirit.

Roland had a local famous and gifted artist, Shirley "Taylor" Gobble, design and create gold cross necklaces with a star in the center for his wife Emilie and each of his four daughters as a way of providing both comfort and a lifelong memory of Taylor. Taylor's art, as well as art by his sisters, has been framed and hung in their home, along with his picture in the family sequence along the wall of the stairwell leading to the bedrooms, and also at the foot of the stairs. So he holds his place within the family conscience.

Families who lose a child have a very high rate of divorce. It has been reported that ninety-five percent of marriages do not survive. One reason is that men and women grieve differently. Men may need more physical closeness, while women tend to become remote from others. Emilie spoke of this difference: she did not want to be touched, nor feel close to anyone again—so that she could never be hurt again.

Emilie's body went into shock. She lost all desire for intimacy. Her daughter, age nineteen, noticed the change in her parents' relationship and two years after Taylor's death told her mother she was concerned. "I'm so worried you won't make it. You don't act the same." Emilie sat Christin down after calling her husband into the room to hear her conversation: "We have changed. I am committed to your dad and the marriage and family for life. No, right now I do not have loving, tingly, warm feelings. But I am committed." Emilie says the marriage survived because of "pure commitment."

Today Emilie describes herself as "the richest person I know." She does not want to sell or move from their house because of all the memories it holds. She loves to hear stories and memories from family and friends about Taylor.

The process of grief has been long and laborious. Almost one year after Taylor's death, Emilie did not want to attend the White Gift Christmas Service at church. At the request of her youngest daughter, Rebecca, Emilie managed to summon the energy and will to attend. The third Christmas after Taylor's death was marked with intense feelings of anger. One year she wrote an article that was published in a religious magazine and in a later year put into a Christmas collection of Christian stories and poems in a special book. The fourth Christmas, her nephew who had witnessed Taylor's death came to see her. It was the first time they had been able to discuss and share together their grief. Shep told her he hadn't wanted to come. She met him at the door, and they fell into each other's arms and sobbed and sobbed together. She did not blame her nephew for Taylor's death, but she had understood how much he struggled to forgive himself for what had happened. Emilie shared how while walking through griefs and pains one must look for miracles. Shep's visit with her was one of those miracles.

Mary, who was so close to Taylor, chose not to talk about Taylor's death for the first two years (each time she did, she would weep). Instead she used her energy to concentrate and focus on her studies. She was the perfect student with high grades. And then, one day, Emilie found her sitting on her bed, staring blankly into space. "What's wrong?" Emilie asked Mary. "I miss my brother," Mary replied. Erupting into deep sobbing, she curled up in her bed. All the pent up anger, hurt, sadness, loss and pain poured out, as if a deep festering wound had broken open. Emilie called Mary's teacher and told her she needed to be taken out of school and allowed time to grieve and heal. She had a test. She was given permission to take it later, but she decided to take it so as to get it over with. Amazingly, she did as well as ever! Emilie had told her, "You are more important than the test." So she slept, cried, and went to lunch with her mother, and took some time to reflect, remember, integrate the loss, and gain a new perspective. Today, Mary is a second-year college student doing well academically, with a bright future. She also takes time for creative self-expression, like being in musicals.

The youngest daughter and sister, Rebecca, can't remember much about the tragedy or her brother. However, she loves hearing stories about Taylor. She also remembers that he paid her a dollar for cleaning his room! Christin, the oldest daughter, graduated from college in the spring as I write, and is considering doing a year with AmeriCorp. Sarah is a rising high school junior. The family feels free to talk about their brother. They continue to heal as they remember him — sharing memories with both laughter and tears! Roland continues in ministry in pastoral care, working with and caring for people who are grieving either due to death or sickness within their families. (In the months after my husband Roy died, it was Roland who called me and delivered to me a Declaration prepared for me by the men of the church who are known as "The Seventy." Roy had been president of their organization at the time of his illness. Their proclamation/remembering was a treasured article — to see how others active in the church saw and remembered my husband. However, such work with grieving people can also be demanding when one is in the throes of one's own personal grief.) Emilie remains a stay-at-home mom, deeply involved in caring for her family and their friends.

Emilie says she has handled her grieving process by talking with anyone and everyone. Besides folding and giving out stars, she also folds a one-dollar bill so it has the shape of a heart with a star in the center. She is thankful that—because of being in the ministry—she and Roland had been exposed to death. She discovered that fifty percent of Taylor's friends in high school had never experienced a death of someone close to them, so she took on the responsibility to open her heart and home to his friends. This became a mission/ministry for her as she also found healing for her pain and loss by bringing new people into her life.

Gifts of notes and things shared from friends returned to her to help in her healing journey. She went to the school and held a "good grief" session for those who knew Taylor to help his young friends grieve.

Nine months after Taylor's death, Emilie's husband Roland was asked to come to Asheville, North Carolina, to conduct a wedding. He wanted her to go with him, but she really didn't want to. But finally she did go. As they traveled she saw and heard "Taylor" everywhere: Taylor Trucking, Taylor Motors, Taylor and Sons, on signs, trucks, TV, radio, at Biltmore Estates. She fell asleep in the car and awakened when they reached a "Taylorsville" sign. The *Touched By an Angel* television show featured a boy named Taylor.

Suddenly Emilie had a blinding insight: "Taylor" was everywhere! He would be with us from now on! He was going to keep giving us signs of his presence within and around us always! In her journal, Emilie wrote: "I don't have to worry about Taylor anymore. He's my safest child." Emilie found this to be a great comfort from God. She confesses she has to guard against being over-protective with her daughters because she fears something might happen to them as well.

Emilie knows people sometimes are reluctant to bring up a loved one and their death, but she has learned—even if remembering brings tears—that grieving is healthy. She appreciates people sharing and remembering Taylor with her. He has become alive once again—in Emilie's heart. Forever!

A mother is the truest friend we have, when trials, heavy and sudden, fall upon us; when adversity takes the place of prosperity; when friends who rejoice with us in our sunshine, desert us when troubles thicken around us, still will she cling to us, and endeavor by her kind precepts and counsels to dissipate the clouds of darkness, and cause peace to return to our hearts.

— Washington Irving

AND GOD SAID

I said, "God, I hurt."
And God said, "I know."

I said, "God, I cry a lot."
And God said, "That is why I gave you tears."

I said, "God, I am so depressed."
And God said, "That is why I gave you loved ones."

I said, "God, my loved one died."
And God said, "So did mine."

I said, "God, it was so violent."
And God said, "I saw mine nailed to a cross."

I said, "God, but your loved one still lives."
And God said, "So does yours."

I said, "God, where are they now?"
And God said, "They are both right here with Me."

I said, "God, it hurts."
And God said, "I know."

— Author unknown

4. How Life is Measured
From an email to RMS by Patti Fisher, quoting Lisa Beamer

Many years ago I had a very special high school teacher whose husband died suddenly of a heart attack. About a week after his death, she shared some of her insight with her students.

As the late afternoon sunlight streamed through our classroom windows, she moved a few things aside on the edge of her desk and sat down there. With a gentle look of reflection she paused and said, "Before class is over, I would like to share with all of you an important thought.

"Each of us is put here on earth to learn, share, love, appreciate others, and give of ourselves. None of us knows when this fantastic experience we call life will end. It can be taken away at any moment. Therefore we must make the most of every single day."

Her eyes began to water but she went on, "So I would like you all to promise me you'll do something. From now on, on your way to school, or on your way home, find something beautiful to notice. It doesn't have to be something you see, it could be small—perhaps the scent of freshly baked bread wafting out of someone's house. Or it could be a sound such as the breeze slightly rustling tree leaves. It might be the glint of morning light on an autumn leaf as it twirls to the ground. Please look for these things, then cherish them. Although it may sound trite, these sights and sounds and smells are the 'stuff' of life, the little things we are put here on earth to enjoy. All too often we take these things for granted. We must make it important to notice them, for at anytime...they can all be taken away."

The class grew quiet. We all picked up our books and silently filed out of the room. That afternoon, I noticed more things on my way home from school than I had that whole semester. Every once in a while, I think of that teacher and remember what an impression she made on all of us, and day by day I try to appreciate all of those things that people sometimes overlook.

Take notice of something special on your lunch hour today. Go barefoot. Or walk on the beach at sunset. Stop off on the way home tonight to get a double dip ice cream cone. As we get older, it is not the things we did that we often regret, but the things we did not do.

The things we see every day are the things we never see at all.

— G. K. Chesterton

A new pastor canvassed the neighborhood. All went well until he came to one house. It was obvious that someone was home, but no one came to the door even after he had knocked several times. Finally, he took out his card, wrote on the back "Revelation 3:20" and stuck it in the door.

The next day after the service, as he was counting the offering, he found his card in the collection plate. Below his message was a notation "Genesis 3:10." Upon opening his Bible to the passage, his face turned red, and he let out a roar of laughter.

Revelation 3:20 reads: "Behold, I stand at the door and knock. If any man hears my voice, and opens the door, I will come in to him, and will dine with him, and he with me."

Genesis 3:10 reads: "And he said, I heard Your voice in the garden, and I was afraid, because I was naked, and I hid myself."

5. Coping with Change
From interviews with friends

In the early 1990s Margaret, a dynamic divorced woman in her 40s, ran a fast-paced travel business and led tours to destinations around the world. She realized, however, that her industry was changing: large corporate franchises were taking over the travel business, squeezing out many of the small independents. Simultaneously, she also realized that she wanted to change her stressful lifestyle and allow herself to enjoy life. It might be time, she thought, to cash in on her hard work by selling out to a larger company. She told her closest friends that she was going to sell her business and change her life. She added that she wanted to find someone to share her life with.

In a different state James, in his mid 50s, was facing similar life choices. He had at that point achieved outstanding professional recognition as a top partner in a national CPA firm. He had done this with long hours, hard work and lots of business travel. In a few years, he knew, he would be forced to retire, because his firm had a mandatory retirement age. The choices he saw included launching a new career, such as becoming a university professor, going into consulting (which could mean losing his retirement benefits), or finding fulfillment by pursuing dreams and interests outside accounting. Divorced for many years while focusing on his career, James had maintained a long-term relationship with a successful doctor in another city. She, however, was not ready to abandon her commitment to her own career and to the status she had achieved within a medical school and in the surrounding community. His continued attempts to negotiate a compromise whereby they could establish a new life together met with rebuffs.

In the course of business travels James and Margaret met. After a period of long-distance interactions, James invited Margaret to visit him at his beach home. Margaret had grown up in California and loved the beach. Living on a beautiful beach was, in fact, part of her inner picture for a lifestyle change.

Both Margaret and James are people who choose to be proactive in life; they both like to create and control outcomes. Over the months following their first meeting they explored their personalities, interests and goals, and looked for areas of common priorities. They created lists of their interests, then gave each interest a ranking. Starting with the premise that both of them wanted and needed to change their lives, they carefully evaluated their compatibility.

They found common ground in both being take-charge, decisive types who were early risers, family oriented, interested in learning to sharpen their intellects, including through world travel. They also discovered that they had mutual commitments to keeping healthy through diet and exercise.

One key latent interest surfaced as well: the game of golf. Neither had yet taken it up but they had both, they found, been thinking about doing so for some time. So golf became another catalyst for their relationship, something that they could learn together and begin playing together.

Margaret sold her travel agency and courageously moved to James's state, storing her personal property for one year. James began his transition from full partner with major leadership responsibilities and constant travel to a new life as an independent consultant. During this period Margaret provided constant emotional support and steady companionship.

During this transition James closed one of the biggest sales his firm had ever experienced. His firm was thus enthusiastic about continuing to work with him as a consultant following his retirement at the mandatory age. Margaret and James exchanged wedding vows in a lovely, simple ceremony at his beach house, surrounded by their families and close friends. Within a short time, they were able to remodel the beach house as a permanent dwelling and move their combined households together.

They joined a country club in their new hometown and undertook the job of improving their golf games. Today, almost a decade since they first made independent decisions to change their lives, they continue to share love, support and companionship, to visit their families, travel, play golf and grow older together. They nurture their minds by taking courses together at a local university. They are a living testimony to the truth that resolving to change a lifestyle, to meet a new partner, to create a whole new life can, with focus and commitment, move from the plane of dreaming and hoping to the level of concrete achievement.

_____

Life is not measured by the number of breaths we take.
It is measured by the moments that take our breath away.

— Author unknown

6. A Christmas Story
Sent to RMS by email, author unknown

In September 1960, I woke up one morning with six hungry babies and just seventy-five cents in my pocket. Their father was gone. The boys ranged from three months to seven years; their sister was two. Their dad had never been much more than a presence they feared. Whenever they heard his tires crunch on the gravel driveway they would scramble to hide under their beds. He did manage to leave fifteen dollars a week to buy groceries. Now that he had decided to leave, there would be no more beatings, but no food either.

If there was a welfare system in effect in southern Indiana at that time, I certainly knew nothing about it. I scrubbed the kids until they looked brand new and then put on my best homemade dress. I loaded them into the rusty old 51 Chevy and drove off to find a job. The seven of us went to every factory, store, and restaurant in our small town. No luck. The kids stayed, crammed into the car and tried to be quiet while I tried to convince whomever would listen that I was willing to learn or do anything. I had to have a job. Still no luck.

The last place we went to, just a few miles out of town, was an old Root Beer Barrel drive-in that had been converted to a truck stop. It was called the Big Wheel.

An old lady named Granny owned the place, and she peeked out the window from time to time at all those kids. She needed someone on the graveyard shift: eleven at night until seven in the morning. She paid sixty-five cents an hour, and I could start that night. I raced home and called the teenager down the street that babysat for people. I bargained with her to come and sleep on my sofa for a dollar a night. She could arrive with her pajamas on and the kids would already be asleep. This seemed like a good arrangement to her, so we made a deal.

That night when the little ones and I knelt to say our prayers we all thanked God for finding Mommy a job. And so I started at the Big Wheel. When I got home in the mornings I woke the babysitter up and sent her home with one dollar of my tip money — fully half of what I averaged every night.

As the weeks went by, heating bills added another strain to my meager wage. The tires on the old Chevy had the consistency of penny balloons and began to leak. I had to fill them with air on the way to work and again every morning before I could go home. One bleak fall morning, I dragged myself to the car to go home and found four tires in the back seat. New tires!

There was no note, no nothing, just those beautiful brand new tires. Had angels taken up residence in Indiana? I wondered. I made a deal with the owner of the local service station. In exchange for his mounting the new tires, I would clean up his office. I remember it took me a lot longer to scrub his floor than it did for him to do the tires.

I was now working six nights instead of five and it still wasn't enough. Christmas was coming, and I knew there would be no money for toys for the kids. I found a can of red paint and started repairing and painting some old toys. Then I hid them in the basement so there would be something for Santa to deliver on Christmas morning. Clothes were a worry, too. I was sewing patches on top of patches on the boys' pants and soon they would be too far gone to repair.

On Christmas Eve the usual customers were drinking coffee in the Big Wheel. These were the truckers, Les, Frank, and Jim, and a state trooper named Joe. A few musicians were hanging around after a gig at the Legion and were dropping nickels in the pinball machine. The regulars all just sat around and talked through the wee hours of the morning and then left to get home before the sun came up.

When it was time for me to go home at seven o'clock on Christmas morning, I hurried to the car. I was hoping the kids wouldn't wake up before I managed to get home and get the presents from the basement and place them under the tree. (We had cut down a small cedar tree by the side of the road down by the dump.) It was still dark and I couldn't see much, but there appeared to be some dark shadows in the car — or was that just a trick of the night? Something certainly looked different, but it was hard to tell what. When I reached the car I peered warily into one of the side windows. Then my jaw dropped in amazement.

My old battered Chevy was filled full to the top with boxes of all shapes and sizes. I quickly opened the driver's side door, scrambled inside, and kneeled in the front facing the back seat. Reaching back, I pulled off the lid of the top box. Inside was a whole case of little blue jeans, sizes two to ten! I looked inside another box: It was full of shirts to go with the jeans. Then I peeked inside some of the other boxes: There were candy and nuts and bananas and bags of groceries. There was an enormous ham for baking and canned vegetables and potatoes. There was pudding and Jell-O and cookies, pie filling and flour. There was a whole bag of laundry supplies and cleaning items. And there were five toy trucks and one beautiful little doll.

As I drove back through empty streets as the sun slowly rose on the most amazing Christmas Day of my life, I was sobbing with gratitude. And I will never forget the joy on the faces of my little ones that precious morning. Yes, there were angels in Indiana that long-ago December. And they all hung out at the Big Wheel truck stop.

7. Love Came Down at Christmas
A story from RMS — Christmas Eve 1995

My husband Roy had run a support group for many years. Since he knew first-hand the pain of going through the holidays without his children, he had always committed to holding meetings of the group during all holiday seasons. Thus members, at their option, could be with understanding people, and not alone, at points of the year meant to be festive. We chose not to go away during such periods in order to serve others who might be hurting. As the first anniversary of Roy's death approached, I determined to follow his example and continue holding the group's meeting at Christmas. This year the usual Sunday night meeting fell on Christmas Eve. My co-leader had gone out of town with his children, so I had to manage the meeting by myself.

I dressed and went to the church parlor where we held our meetings. I was early. A profound sense of loss permeated my being. Bravely, with a sense of deep commitment to the memories of the work Roy had so passionately nurtured, I waited for members to arrive. I tried to prepare to listen and respond with as much love and support as I could muster. Only one person showed up. He was usually one of the quiet members of the group. Like me, he had no children from his marriage and no family in town. He, too, was alone.

We waited for others to arrive, making small talk. But no one else came. At first haltingly, and later, with laughter and tears, I shared my memories of Christmas Eve 1994, the night that Roy died. I talked about the profound spiritual love we felt for each other, the pain of losing him "too soon," my grief over my hopes and dreams for growing old together being dashed. I went on about how Roy had made me understand something of God's love, my conviction that we truly were soul mates. The lone support group member who had showed up became my healer. He listened with great attention as I poured out my heart about the love I had known and had lost.

About 10 p.m., before he went home, my listener walked with me to the sanctuary of the church for the annual Christmas Eve service so that I did not have to walk there alone. Very few people had arrived. I sat down beside a woman who had been in one of Roy's groups. It was almost as if God knew I needed people around me who could understand how much I missed my husband, especially at Christmas.

What was hard was realizing that exactly at this point a year ago I had sat with Bob Nations, a friend, at Roy's bedside as Roy made the passage from physical life here on earth to life in his home in the spiritual world beyond. Somehow I made it through the service.

As the service ended, a woman I knew by sight but had never met personally turned to me. We introduced ourselves. When I said my name, this woman, Emilie Barnhardt, reached over and hugged me. Then she reached under the bench and brought up a little loaf of home-baked bread. It had a tiny, perfectly formed Moravian star attached to it. She said, "This is for your breakfast in the morning." The love and care she radiated was palpable. Deeply touched, I broke into sobs. My protected social façade had been overcome by her compassion.

I explained, with some embarrassment, that my husband had died a year earlier. She told me that her husband Roland had already told her that. I could not stop sobbing. As Roland waited patiently in the aisle, Emilie invited me home to spend the night with her family. She assured me that they had "plenty of room," and that their children would love having me enjoy Christmas morning with them!

In my mind danced visions of "crashing" a family party, and besides, I had been invited to spend Christmas with dear friends Diane and Bob Nations, so I declined Emilie's generous offer. But her reaching out to me so lovingly touched me deeply. Suddenly, all I wanted to do was to run away and work through my feelings. Receiving so much love in one night was almost more than I knew how to bear.

Somehow I made it to my car and drove home safely, sobbing the whole way. As I drove I talked out loud to Roy. I told him how much I missed him and still loved him. At home I crawled into bed and cried myself to sleep. Hours later I woke up feeling renewed, and joined the Nations family for a loving, laughing family Christmas celebration. I felt at peace again. And I was surprised by the joy singing in my heart.

Christ was born anew for me between that Christmas Eve and the wonderful Christmas Day that followed.

Frogs

Sent by email from Maureen Stahle and William Hanson

I was told a story about a lady in the hospital who was near death when an area chaplain came to visit her. This chaplain was a very young female with long blonde hair. She listened to the lady who was ill and left her a small gift for comfort. It was a tiny ceramic frog.

The next day one of the people from the lady's church came to visit. The lady told her friend about the beautiful young chaplain who had come to visit her. The friend was so impressed with the way the lady had improved and felt the need to talk to the young chaplain.

In her search to find the young gal, she was repeatedly reassured that the chaplains are never very young and that there was never a gal that fit the description given. Upon returning to the lady in the hospital, a visiting nurse entered the room and noticed the ceramic frog. The nurse made the comment, "I see you have a guardian angel with you," as she held the little frog. We asked why she made the comment and we were informed that the frog stood for: (F) Fully (R) Rely (O) On (G) God.

8. The Bridge
From Bob Proctor's *Daily Insights*

Once upon a time two brothers who lived on adjoining farms fell into conflict. It was the first serious rift in forty years of farming side by side; sharing machinery and trading labor and goods as needed had always gone without a hitch. Then the longtime collaboration fell apart. It began with a small misunderstanding, grew into a major difference, and finally exploded into an exchange of bitter words. Weeks of silence followed.

One morning there was a knock on John's door. He opened it to find a man with a carpenter's toolbox. "I am looking for a few days' work," he said. "Perhaps you would have a few small jobs here and there I could help with?" "Yes," said the older brother. "I do have a job for you. Look across the creek at the farm, that's my neighbor; in fact, it's my younger brother. Last week there was a meadow between us, and he took his bulldozer to the river levee and now there is a creek between us. Well, he may have done this to spite me, but I'll do him one better. See that pile of lumber by the barn? I want you to build me a fence — an eight foot fence — so I won't need to see his place or his face anymore."

The carpenter said, "I think I understand the situation. Show me the nails and the post hole digger and I'll be able to do a job that pleases you." The older brother had to go to town, so he helped the carpenter get the materials ready. Then he was off for the day. The carpenter worked hard all day, measuring, sawing, and nailing. About sunset when the farmer returned, the carpenter had just finished his job. The farmer's eyes opened wide; his jaw dropped. There was no fence there at all — the finished structure was a bridge stretching from one side of the creek to the other! A fine piece of work, handrails and all — and the neighbor, his younger brother, was approaching the bridge, his hands outstretched. "You are quite a fellow to build this bridge after all I have said and done," the younger brother said. The two brothers stood at each end of the bridge and then walked toward each other to meet in the middle. Taking each other's hand, they turned to see the carpenter hoist his toolbox on his shoulder. "No, wait! Stay a few days. I've got lots of projects for you," said the older brother.

"I'd love to stay on," the carpenter replied, "but I have more bridges to build."

See www.rhodasearcy.com.

9. Changing Perceptions and Paradigms
A Story told by Rick Seymour, a motivational trainer

In Australia there is a six-hundred kilometer foot race from Sidney to Melbourne. It is long, tough, and takes five days to run. This race makes marathons look easy!

Cliff Young showed up in 1988, wearing overalls and galoshes over work boots. Cliff was sixty-one years old. No one knew he was planning to run. He joined 150 world-class athletes. Now this is a Big Race with Big Sponsors, like Nike. Racers are eighteen to twenty year olds — men and women — who run endurance races all over the world.

So that day, when Cliff walked up to get his number, it was apparent he planned to run. People watching thought it was a publicity stunt. Who's sponsoring him? Who's backing him? They thought he'd drop out in thirty minutes. After all, he was sixty-one years old. No one ran that race at sixty-one! And wearing overalls? Rubber galoshes? This was nuts! Cliff picked up his number: sixty-four.

The press got curious. They watched him move into position within the pack wearing expensive racing gear. They put mikes in his face. "Who are you? Where are you going?"

"I'm Cliff Young. I'm from a large ranch outside Melbourne where we run sheep."

"You're really going to run?"

"Yeah."

"Got any backers?"

"No."

"Then you can't run."

"Yeah, I can," Cliff replied. "You see, I grew up on a farm where we couldn't afford horses or four-wheel drives. And the whole time I was growing up until about four years ago, when we finally made some money and got a four-wheeler. But the storms would come up and I'd have to go out and round up the sheep. We had two thousand head and two thousand acres. Sometimes we'd have to run those sheep for two to three days. Took a long time, but I'd catch them! I believe I can run this race — it's only two more days: five days! I run sheep for three."

When Cliff started the race with all these young world-class athletes, people shouted: "Someone stop him! He'll die! He's crazy!" They broadcast it over the news immediately, and all of Australia was watching this crazy guy as he shuffled along in galoshes.

The existing paradigm for the race was to run eighteen hours and sleep six. But Cliff didn't stop after eighteen hours. He kept running. Every night he got a bit closer to the front. By the last night he passed them. By the last day he was way out in front of them. Not only did he run the Sidney race at age sixty-one, without collapsing, he won first place by nine hours and became a national hero!

When he finished the race, the media asked what he thought and what he had done to win. Cliff didn't know you were supposed to sleep. His paradigm was chasing sheep, trying to outrun a storm. With every conceivable limitation against him, Cliff changed the whole paradigm of that race. Now no one sleeps!

To win that race, you have to run all night as well as all day. And it's really funny: the last three winners of the race have used the Cliff Young shuffle, because it's more efficient than the way the world-class runners were running before.

To win in life's storms, often we have to change our paradigms — and refuse to let limitations stop us. Cliff used life experience and transferred it to a new situation. That type of creative thinking and positive belief in oneself is critical to seeing change and crises as an opportunity to achieve and accomplish, to transform oneself.

10. "You Are My Sunshine"
A story sent to RMS by Courtney Thompson via email

Like any good mother, when Karen found out that another baby was on the way, she did what she could to help her three-year-old son, Michael, prepare for a new sibling. They found out that the new baby was going to be a girl, and day after day, night after night, Michael sang to his sister in mommy's tummy. He was building a bond of love with his little sister before he even met her. The pregnancy progressed normally for Karen, an active member of the Panther Creek United Methodist Church in Morristown, Tennessee. In time, the labor pains came. Soon it was every five minutes, every three, every minute.

But serious complications arose during delivery and Karen found herself in hours of labor. Would a C-section be required? Finally, after a long struggle, Michael's little sister was born. But she was in very serious condition. With a siren howling in the night, the ambulance rushed the infant to the neonatal intensive care unit at St. Mary's Hospital, Knoxville, Tennessee.

The days inched by. The little girl got worse. The pediatrician had to tell the parents there was very little hope. Be prepared for the worst. Karen and her husband contacted a local cemetery about a burial plot. They had fixed up a special room in their house for their new baby, but now they found themselves having to plan for a funeral. Michael, however, kept begging his parents to let him see his sister. "I want to sing to her," he kept saying. Week two in Intensive Care looked as if a funeral would come before the week was over. Michael kept nagging about singing to his sister, but kids are never allowed in Intensive Care.

Karen decided to take Michael whether they liked it or

not. If he didn't see his sister right then, he may never see her alive. She dressed him in an oversized scrub suit and marched him into ICU. He looked like a walking laundry basket. The head nurse recognized him as a child and bellowed: "Get that kid out of here now. No children are allowed."

The mother rose up strong in Karen, and the usually mild-mannered lady glared steel-eyed right into the head nurse's face, her lips a firm line. "He is not leaving until he sings to his sister," she stated. Then Karen towed Michael to his sister's bedside. He gazed at the tiny infant losing the battle to live. After a moment, he began to sing. In the pure-hearted voice of a three-year-old, Michael sang: "You are my sunshine, my only sunshine, you make me happy when skies are gray."

Instantly the baby girl seemed to respond. The pulse rate began to calm down and become steady. "Keep on singing, Michael," encouraged Karen with tears in her eyes.

"You never know, dear, how much I love you, please don't take my sunshine away."

As Michael sang to his sister, the baby's ragged, strained breathing became as smooth as a kitten's purr. "Keep on singing, sweetheart."

"The other night, dear, as I lay sleeping, I dreamed I held you in my arms."

Michael's little sister began to relax as rest, healing rest, seemed to sweep over her. "Keep on singing, Michael." Tears had now conquered the face of the bossy head nurse. Karen glowed.

"You are my sunshine, my only sunshine. Please don't take my sunshine away...." The next day...the very next day...the little girl was well enough to go home. *Woman's Day* magazine called it "The Miracle of a Brother's Song." The medical staff just called it a miracle. Karen called it a miracle of God's love.

11. Losing a Spouse, Loving and Marrying Again

For forty-seven years Ruth lived as a minister's wife in a small southern town. She and her husband Huitt, whom she loved dearly, had two daughters while he pastored a total of eight churches. One Sunday while the minister was preaching from Revelations 4:1, Huitt had a heart attack. Transported urgently to the hospital, much to Ruth's shock and dismay, he was pronounced dead.

After mourning, with support from her daughters and friends, and her strong faith, Ruth decided she would conquer grief, with help from God. Her formula was travel and gardening. She took a number of trips in the United States and Europe with close single female friends, and also nurtured a garden with beautiful flowers, which she found very healing and restoring. She likewise nurtured the spiritual growth of other women in teaching a Sunday School class for fifteen years.

In another town a few hours away, James, a man in his mid eighties, with five grown children, was grieving the death of her wife of sixty-two years. He was a successful landscape designer and businessman. When his wife died, he described his feelings as "numb." Never had he felt so alone. These feelings came as a huge shock to James. He needed someone to fill the terrible void.

Both Ruth and James had children who were involved in art, so they were invited to an art show at Ruth's daughter's gallery. They met around Thanksgiving, a year after James's wife died. Something magical happened. Ruth said they first became friends and then fell in love. His being a Christian man was important to her, and she acknowledged "the chemistry was right". He, on the other hand, could not forget her sparkling blue eyes. So he "tracked her down" to her home where he found her in the midst of her flower garden.

They had their first date six weeks after meeting. They went to see the Christmas lights at Tanglewood Park outside Winston-Salem. Ruth had been feeling that she needed to give up her lovely home with her collected antiques and several acres of flowers because it "was becoming a millstone around her neck". They both believed a "Higher Power" orchestrated this meeting and relationship. When James came to visit at her church, her minister announced their relationship from the pulpit and meant it as an affirmation. Her friends were amazed that she had a serious male friend! As they continued to date, they learned they had deep common interests—their Christian faith, flowers and plants, and horses. James had taught all his grandchildren to ride; Ruth's father had bred Tennessee Walking horses.

One day, James said to Ruth:" Come and grow old with me. The best is yet to be." Ruth asked, "Is that a proposal?" And James responded: "Yes! That's the best I can do!" So in the spring they were married in a simple wedding.

Ruth has adopted the Biblical character Ruth's philosophy: "Your people shall be my people and your God my God. Where you go, I will go." She has warmly embraced James' family by saying she "inherited thirty-four members of an extended family" and they "all accepted me graciously." Ruth describes James as a "Southern gentleman." A gracious and generous woman, Ruth gave up her home and community, and asked her daughters to divide her treasures between them, and sell what they did not want. She wept when she saw her empty house. She discovered that even in good change, it is possible to experience some grief as one lets go of the old and moves forward in faith. She enjoys seeing her daughters have her treasures in their homes where she can still see them. She laughs when they tell her she cannot take her treasures back!

12. Changing the World Through Vision and Leadership

(Adapted from *From the Field*, and two videos on Dr. Shaklee: "To Share a Dream" and "The Dream Continues" by Shaklee Corporation 1981, The Silver Jubilee 25 Years of History.) This article has not been endorsed by the Shaklee Corporation.

Dr. Forrest C. Shaklee wrote: "I have spent my life studying the ways and secrets of Nature. She is a wise and noble teacher. Humbly trying to learn and follow her truths has made my life rich, fulfilling and exciting. I hope that some of the thoughts and products I have developed in my half-century study will be of meaning and value to you and those you care about."

The Shaklee story began as the visionary leadership of one man. Dr. Shaklee was many decades ahead of his time. He understood the connection between good health, good nutrition, and God's creation. Almost a century ago — early in the twentieth century — he developed a philosophy of achieving optimum health through being in harmony with nature. His beliefs and actions built a grass roots health revolution, wellness focus, and advanced method of distribution for consumer products years ahead of the norm.

Who would have dreamed when Forrest was born on an icy November day in the late nineteenth century outside the small town of Carlisle, Iowa, that this sickly baby would grow up to become a man who would change the world? Not even his doctor believed he would live. However, the doctor allowed his mother to nurse him out of pity. He was born consumptive, and many of his peers died with tuberculosis. His mother and grandmother used their knowledge of good nutrition and wild herbs to provide Forrest with the raw ingredients to strengthen his sickly body. Observing nature during the countless hours he spent outside in the fresh air and sunshine fed his curious, active mind. Forrest supplied the inner courage and will to live as he observed nature's regenerative ways. From that early childhood influence and experiences, a life long interest in nature's balance, beauty, and bounty was born. Exposure to some of the great thinkers and orators of his day when they became guests in his family's home expanded his ideological creativity and philosophical talents, providing him with mentors and role models for leadership in his adult life.

His interest in nature led him to study health and the body and then on to the, at that time, new science of chiropractic medicine. He established a chiropractic practice, financing its beginnings by passionately persuading a banker that the wealth within his mind made him a viable candidate for a loan. He began to see the importance of integrating all the disciplines of medicine to enhance patient treatment, now known as the holistic health or complementary medicine movement. He was truly a pioneer in the wellness industry emerging today. As he treated his patients, he was able to correlate their health with their eating habits.

He was an avid follower of the work of Casimir Funk, a famous nutrition researcher who pioneered the discovery of vitamins. Studying Funk's work led him to the realization that if he could stabilize the minerals extracted from vegetable sources, he could create a substance that might be used for the prevention of nutritional disorders and promote health and wellness.

When he was able to do this, he called his product "vitalized minerals." Thus was born the product that eventually became known as VitaLea Multivitamin and Multi-mineral Supplement. Dr. Shaklee became overexposed to radiation from the then-new technology of x-raying bones, and developed cancer. His own doctor wanted to amputate his affected arm to prevent the spread and prolong his life, but Dr. Shaklee refused, emphatically declaring he would not die! He took a sabbatical from his practice for several years and returned to his roots to nurture himself with pure wholesome food, sunshine, exercise, and meditation within nature. Eventually, he was able to return to his clinical practice. He lived into his nineties, active, healthy, and contributing to society.

Dr. Shaklee's reputation grew along with his clientele. His active creative mind and wide-ranging interests brought him into contact with some of the great men of his day. Thomas Edison, an inventor who had little interest in meeting people, asked to meet Dr. Shaklee, who invented one of the first travel home vehicles. Later, through Edison, Dr. Shaklee met Henry Ford and Harvey Firestone. Dr. Shaklee knew loss and change and human tragedy. His first wife, the mother of his two sons, died; eventually he married his beloved "Dorothy," who became his help mate and companion in his business. Dorothy died after Dr. Shaklee, in her mid-nineties, less than a decade ago. Dr. Shaklee's clinic also burned to the ground and much of his early nutritional research and clinical data was lost in the flames. He moved to Florida and eventually California, settling in the San Francisco area. But he never stopped dreaming and achieving.

In the 1940s he retired from clinic work and devoted his time to lecturing on nutrition and his personal philosophy of thoughtmanship. Then, in his early sixties, instead of slipping away into retirement, he decided to start a company with his two sons, Forrest, Jr. and Raleigh, to distribute his nutritional supplements to patients and others who heard him speak and learned of their health benefits. This enterprise became the Shaklee Corporation founded in 1956, and is currently the wellness subsidiary of Yamanouchi, one of the world's largest international pharmaceutical companies. The Japanese owners envisioned the long-term trends in health care in the late 1980s and wanted an established, clinically research-based wellness focused nutritional supplement company as part of their organization. Shaklee's solid foundation of science-based, clinically tested and peer reviewed products combined with the best of nature (whole food based) was the winner, and a great partnership was begun. Dr. Shaklee's humble beginnings and powerful philosophy to be in harmony with nature in the heartland of the United States birthed an international success story. (I often marvel how Iowa was the birthplace of both Dr. Shaklee and another visionary: Dr. Robert H. Schuler, who established the longest televised Christian broadcast, the Hour of Power, with its positive message of love and hope around the world.)

★ ★ ★ ★ ★ ★ ★

Following his retirement, Dr. Shaklee had frequently been approached for the nutritional supplements he had distributed through his clinics. Although there was an established need for his products, distribution was a problem since his clinics no longer were operating. He made the decision to ensure quality and freshness of the products by offering a business marketing opportunity for those who believed in his products. He especially was interested in the potential within the human being. He desired to find a way to market his products that allowed others to leverage his expertise and knowledge in the development of products and to create synergy, plussing the products with a dynamic, new, rewarding marketing and distribution independent business opportunity of their own. Dr. Shaklee's creative vision helped start a new product distribution method which has since spread around the world. In the nutritional supplement business, Shaklee has survived and grown and changed over its forty-five year history. But its founding principles of Living in Harmony with nature and abiding by the Golden Rule (Do unto others as you would have them do unto you) are as relevant today as they were forty-five years ago. Dr. Shaklee's concern for and reverence regarding nature's healing power and protecting the environment which can heal us remain fundamental truths in the twenty-first century. In fact, Shaklee Corporation was the first company certified as climate neutral at the turn of the twenty-first century. The Shaklee Corporation is known for its integrity, its reliance on clinical research in product development, its highest of standards for safety, bio availability, and quality control from raw ingredients to distribution and its care for the environment. The products and the business have changed thousands of lives for almost half a century. In a world that needs a new paradigm for health care and wellness for humans and the environment, Shaklee stands as a beacon of light and hope, lighting the way to both health and wealth for everyday ordinary people.

I never belittle the medical profession, but we are two separate fields of endeavor. They are trained to treat disease. I'm interested in building health.

The road to health, happiness and fulfillment is found in Nature. Our only task is to follow it, stopping along the way to learn Nature's secrets and enjoy her fruits.

— Dr. Forrest C. Shaklee, Sr.

13. Coping with Multiple Losses with Faith and Resiliency

A story shared by my Aunt Miriam Longacre in words, letters, and from a Memoriam article written by Nancy Whitmer.

Miriam was born and raised in Lancaster County, Pennsylvania, where extended family ties and relationships are the fabric of Mennonite and Amish culture. She had experienced the grief of losing parents after chronic illnesses. Her father, Harry, a very happy person by nature, sang hymns of faith in the hospital, such as "We are going down the valley one by one, human comrades, you and I will be one," and "Take my life and let it be consecrated, Lord, to thee. Take my moments and my days, let them flow in ceaseless praise." Her father's doctor wanted to amputate his leg to resolve problems caused by arteriosclerosis. Both he and his family decided against the surgery, and he was moved to a nursing home for care. The night before Easter, Miriam visited him and quoted the 23rd Psalm (The Lord is my Shepherd) to him. On Easter Sunday, he died. His granddaughter Rhoda, age sixteen, was away at Lancaster Mennonite School and had to write an English composition, which was very difficult for her. However, she ended up writing a poem:

I am thinking of you, Grandma,
As I write this little rhyme.
Many years you had with Grandpa,
Yet it was just a short, short time.
Grandpa dear has gone before us
How we miss his smiling face
And in all the years that follow,
None will ever take his place.

But we know our Heavenly Father
Plans our lives for our own good.
So we pray in deep submission,
May Thy will be done, Oh Lord.
God will slowly ease the heartache
And will wipe the tears away,
As we toil on toward evening
To that Land of Endless Day.

At this writing, Miriam is in her mid eighties. Her heart has been touched with pain and joy, grief and celebration. Her sister Anna had lovingly cared for a retarded niece until she became ill. Her illness left her suffering in her last days. After Anna's death, Miriam found a piece of paper in her sister's Bible, written in her handwriting. Entitled: "What He has done for me." She read this at Anna's funeral:

His eye sees me.	*His arm reaches me.*
His ear hears me.	*His blood washes me.*
His heart loves me.	*His Spirit leads me.*
His voice calls me.	*His Word comforts me.*
His Hand holds me.	*His presence goes with me.*

Finding this, and sharing it with the family, Miriam discovered was a big comfort to the whole family.

She also considers it a privilege that she took care of prior to and witnessed the deaths of her mother and father-in-law, and her own mother. Hearing their testimonies of faith and trust in God gave her comfort and helped her accept their deaths. Having these intimate experiences with death and dying and deep faith while younger became preparations for what she was going to face — unbeknown to her — in the future that would rock any human.

On March 28, 1986, Miriam and her husband Daniel

faced the biggest challenge of their lives.

As Chuck Brubaker drove home from Good Friday evening services, he had no way of knowing that just ahead the rural road was blocked by a piece of disabled machinery. Without warning, his car slammed into the immovable object, and the wrenching sounds of metal crunching against metal shattered the tranquility of the soft spring night.

For Chuck and his wife, Joyce, a disc harrow, designed to prepare soil for new life, became an instrument of death. Joyce, thirty-two, died in the ambulance on the way to the hospital; Charles, better known as Chuck, also thirty-two, died the next day without regaining consciousness.

Chuck, Joyce, and their two children, Eric, nearly five, and Carmen, thirteen months, had looked forward to spending Easter weekend with Joyce's parents, Miriam and Daniel Longacre, in Franklin County, Pennsylvania. The Brubakers left their Lancaster County home on Good Friday morning, did some sightseeing along the way, and arrived at Joyce's home in time for supper.

That evening, the Brubakers accompanied their parents to church. After the service, before leaving the church, Joyce dressed Carmen in her pajamas, and Chuck gave his daughter a kiss.

Grandma Miriam Longacre took Eric in her car; Grandpa Daniel Longacre went with his daughter and son-in-law. The accident occurred several miles from the church. Little Carmen, who was strapped into her car seat, escaped serious injury. Daniel was hospitalized with bruises and fractures.

The Brubakers' friends and relatives reacted to the news of the accident with shocked disbelief.

"Chuck and Joyce were so young," one friend said. "They were needed by their family, friends, and their world."

"We remember Chuck and Joyce for their loving, gentle

commitment to the things that matter," another friend observed.

One of the things that mattered to the Brubakers was their family. Although Chuck was caretaker at Woodcrest, a Christian day camp near Ephrata, Pennsylvania, and taught seventh and eighth grades at Hinkletown Mennonite School, he spent time with the children each evening before they went to bed. Sometimes, Eric went to school with his father and played on Chuck's computer.

During the night after the accident, Eric went into the Intensive Care Unit to see his Daddy. He put out his little hand and said: "He was my best friend." One of Eric's treasured possessions is Chuck's Bible, which he sometimes carries to church. Carmen, listening to a tape recording of Chuck talking, said about the father she doesn't remember: "He sounds like a kind man."

Joyce, too, gave the family priority. A registered nurse, she put her career on hold after Carmen's birth so she could be at home with the children. In her quiet, unassuming way, Joyce gave love and support to the children and Chuck.

Eric went along when Chuck's parents Lester and Lois Brubaker chose a tombstone for his daddy and mommy. "It should say something about love," Eric suggested. (On the tombstone is a heart-shaped section with "Love" written on it, with Eric and Carmen's names engraved along the edges.)

Immediately after the accident, the children stayed with Chuck's parents, Miriam and Daniel, then approaching seventy, and Daniel was recovering from multiple fractures in the accident. Within weeks, however, the children went to live with Chuck's sister and her husband, Rose and Chris Kennel. The Kennels lovingly accepted Eric and Carmen into their home and adopted them in 1987. The bonding between the Kennels and the children was especially precious, because the Kennels too had experienced a loss. Their only son was stillborn several years previously. Their extended families were also important to Chuck and Joyce.

Chuck's death was especially hard for his father. "Chuck was my first-born son," Lester explained. "Also, he was following in my footsteps professionally. I saw Chuck achieving in his life some of the goals I had wanted for my own but had never attained. Even though I was Chuck's father, I felt that I was looking up to him."

Lester also remembers his son's positive outlook on life. "Chuck had a tremendous sense of humor," Lester said. "But he was never sarcastic. I don't remember ever hearing Chuck speak in a derogatory way about anyone."

Lester and Lois agree that Chuck was an ideal son except for his junior year in high school. He chose — as can happen during teen years — to be friends with classmates who were rebelling and getting into trouble. After a talk with the school principal and his parents, Chuck made new choices. Later he said, "I don't know why I acted like that."

Chuck was almost eight years old when his only brother, Ed, was born. "I can't wait until he's old enough to get into my things," Chuck said, not reflecting the usual sentiments of an older brother. The two brothers always got along well.

When Ed wanted to do something in memory of his brother, he proposed a scholarship in Chuck and Joyce's name. As a result, the Charles R. and Joyce A. Longacre Brubaker Scholarship Fund was established to aid Eastern Mennonite College (now University) students studying education and nursing. Another scholarship has been established at Eastern Mennonite High School where Chuck graduated. (And in Spring 2002, Carmen Brubaker Kennel was an honor student and junior at Lancaster Mennonite High School, where my sister-in-law, Jane Moyer, teaches English.)

In addition to family, other people were important to Chuck and Joyce. Joyce was an empathetic and sensitive person. After graduating from college, she worked on the pediatrics ward at Hershey Medical Center. She loved the babies and liked to relate to their families, but found the job difficult. Many of the desperately ill children did not recover, and Joyce had a hard time dealing with that pain and tragedy.

Chuck was a dedicated teacher interested in his students' lives both in and out of the classroom. He had high expectations for his students, and they rewarded him by stretching to meet those expectations. After his death, the students at Hinkletown dedicated their yearbook to Chuck.

Joyce received all her education at Mennonite schools. Six days before the accident, she spoke at the annual meeting of the Lancaster Mennonite Conference. "I don't feel that I've led a sheltered life because I've had an exclusively Mennonite education," Joyce said. "I feel strongly that a Christian education should not be used as an escape from the world and its realities. Rather, it is an opportunity for students to equip themselves for reaching out into the world." While students at Eastern Mennonite College, Chuck and Joyce both reached out to the world by serving with an Ocean City, Maryland, boardwalk ministry for runaways and other troubled youth.

Chuck and Joyce graduated from Eastern Mennonite College in 1975 and 1976 respectively, and they married in 1977. Two years later they went to Buffalo, New York, where they served as unit leaders in a voluntary service household. After two years, they stayed in Buffalo so Chuck could earn his master's degree. Eric had been born in Buffalo.

When the Brubakers moved back to Lancaster County in 1982, they returned to Chuck's home congregation, First

Deaf Mennonite. Joyce worked part time in a nursing home, and Chuck taught at Hinkletown Mennonite School. In 1983, they moved to a mobile home at Woodcrest Camp and additionally served as its caretakers until their deaths.

Chuck and Joyce modeled a life of simplicity and contentment. They loved the Lord and other people far more than they cared for things. The Brubakers tried to be good stewards of their material possessions, but the accumulation of money was never a driving motivation for them.

After the accident, Chuck's Bible and a scrap of paper were found in the wrecked car. On the paper, in Chuck's neat handwriting and possibly written at that last Good Friday service, were the words, "For me to live is Christ and to die is gain."

Hanging across the front of Chuck's classroom at Hinkletown was a banner that he designed on his computer. It read: "What you are is God's Gift to you; what you become is your Gift to God."

During their short thirty-two years, Chuck and Joyce became sensitive and loving people who served God by serving others. Their lives touched many — the patients Joyce cared for, the inquiring minds Chuck challenged, and the family, friends, and acquaintances they loved. Chuck and Joyce Brubaker were committed to things that mattered.

Seven years later, Miriam and Daniel Longacre were attending a Sweetheart's Banquet at their church. Miriam wrote a poem as a surprise to share with Daniel and the others that night. In the poem, she addressed the great loss of their daughter Joyce and son-in-law Chuck.

In response to my inquiry of how they coped with such a shocking double death, she shared how Chuck's written note in his Bible gave her/them great comfort (To die is gain), as well as the cards and letters from many people whose lives had been touched by Chuck and Joyce because "they lived a life that mattered." Also, she said that many prayers were prayed throughout all the counties in Pennsylvania, Virginia, and New York, and this helped to ease their sorrow and heal the wound. And she said, "Nothing with God is accidental." Such is her deep faith. Arnold Schwarzenegger said, "Strength does not come from winning. Your struggles develop your strengths. When you go through hardships and decide not to surrender, that is strength." Miriam's strength and courage and faith were about to be tested even more greatly.

Ten years after their children's death, in December 1996, another tragedy (from a human perspective) happened. Daniel and Miriam had just returned to their home in rural southwestern Pennsylvania, after visiting family and friends in central and eastern Pennsylvania for several days. Miriam was driving and had dropped Daniel off to pick up the mail at the roadside mailbox. He had crossed the road to check for mail. She waited in the car in their drive. When he did not return, she got out and began to look for him. He was not at the mailbox, so she continued to look for him, walking down the road. She discovered a leg lying on the road, and then further on, another leg. Also some clothes that had been ripped off of him. Then she saw a car stopped down the road a little distance, and a woman walking toward her.

The woman spoke: "I hit him. I thought I hit a deer." In shock, Miriam said, "Yes, you did hit a dear."

He had landed on the hood of her car, and his head hit and shattered her windshield. Seeing his face made her realize it was a person, not a deer.

The ambulance was called to get him. Later, the funeral director told her every bone in Daniel's body had been broken. Both her daughter and daughter-in-law advised her not to look at his body, but she insisted she needed to see him, and at the least be able to put her hand inside the casket and touch him. So the funeral director used all his skill to hide the damage so she could view him. But he told her there could not be a viewing of the body the next day because by that time his appearance would not be good enough for others to view.

Miriam shares some of her thoughts about how she coped: "Faith draws the poison from every grief, and takes the sting from every loss. God is our refuge and strength, a very present help in trouble." Miriam expresses gratitude for having memorized scripture (the Bible) which now come to mind at times like this when she needs them. She especially likes: "For we know that if our earthly house of this tabernacle be dissolved, we have a building of God, a house not made with hands eternal in the heavens." II Corinthians 5:1.

*   *   *   *   *   *   *

A very significant part of Mennonite culture is music, beautiful a cappella singing in four-part harmony, always a part of church, family, and social occasions. And so another source of comfort and healing for her has been words of Christian hymns: "Precious memories, how they linger, how they ever flood my soul; In the stillness of the midnight...while the ceaseless ages roll." Writing poetry has also been a creative way to express feelings and grief, and share with others.

After Daniel's death, Miriam decided to sell her home, because she could not stand to live there, where the memories of the horror and pain of that night would constantly be triggered and replayed as scenes in her mind and emotions. She decided to move to the Fairmount Retirement Home in Ephrata, Pennsylvania. Her physical, spiritual, and financial needs have been met. She has a nice big room with three windows facing the beautiful farm land of Lancaster County where she was born and raised. In the past, her room was one of several that were in the nursing section before it was remodeled. Her daughter Joyce had walked the halls and given care to others in that building before her death. So she cherishes her memories of Joyce and feels Joyce's spirit of love and is content. In addition, her older sister (also a widow) joined her and lived in the apartment next door from December 1998 until her death in May 2002.

Remember Miriam said, "There are no accidents with God"? One Sunday after Daniel's tragic death, Miriam and one of her sons went to their former church to visit. A visiting minister from the Menno Haven Nursing Home was preaching the message. He told how his own son had died suddenly and the effect it had had on him. At the close of the message, he asked if anyone had anything to say. Miriam stood up and asked if it was wrong to ask "Why?" when there was a sudden death in the family. He responded, no, it was not wrong. So at the close of the service she again stood up and asked the congregation to pray for her as she was sorry, but she had a "wrong attitude" and held it against the woman who killed her husband. She acknowledged the woman had not done it on purpose, it had been an accident and the other woman was also suffering, and had to live with the thoughts that she had caused a man's death. After Miriam shared her feelings and pain with the congregation, a peace came over her and she knew God had forgiven her for her attitudes. She felt a sense of forgiveness and inner peace and harmony.

Miriam also related how her daughter Rhoda (my cousin) came to spend the night with her at their home after Daniel's accident and death. Miriam slept in one bedroom and Rhoda in another. During the night Miriam was crying and Rhoda heard her and came into her room and put her arms around her to comfort her. She told her they should be thankful that the Lord had taken Daniel, because if he had lived, he would have been in a vegetable state and very difficult to care for. Miriam was then eighty. So, that knowledge comforted her and allowed her to release him, as she grieved.

Miriam shared a poem given her by a friend:

Should You Go First

Should you go first, and I remain, to walk the road alone,
I'll live in memory's garden, dear, with happy days
    we've known.
In spring, I'll wait for roses red, when fades the lilac blue,
In early Fall, when brown leaves call, I'll catch a glimpse
    of you.

Should you go first, and I remain, for battles to be fought,
Each thing you've touched along the way will be
    a hallowed spot.
I'll hear your voice, I'll see your smile,
Though blindly I may grope;
The memory of your helping hand, will buoy me
    on with hope.

Should you go first, and I remain, to finish with the scroll
No lengthening shadows shall creep in
To make this life seem droll.
We've known so much of happiness, we've had
    our cup of joy,
And memory is one Gift of God, that death cannot destroy.

— A.K. Roswell

When Miriam's sister Ruth died recently and I called to speak to her a few weeks after the funeral, she told me how she missed playing Scrabble with Ruth. Then she added that she had had a visit from a cousin's children and they promised to return and play with her in the future. Courageously she said, "There is always someone to come along...." Perhaps this is a secret to surviving grief: continuing to open up to new possibilities and new relationships.

Author's note: Miriam is my aunt, married to Daniel who was my mother's brother, closest in age to her. Miriam was like a sister to my mother. My mother had died a little over a month previous to this event. Miriam and Daniel had just come from visiting my newly widowed Dad — as well as other friends and family in that area. My own grief over losing my husband Roy less than two years previously and my mother a little over a month earlier made this event especially touching and painful.

Some information for this story came from a brochure written by Nancy Whitmer after Chuck and Joyce's deaths.

The poem, "What He has done for me" was changed to all present tense verbs.

What is dying?

From the hospice booklet "Gone from My Sight" by Barbara Kames. A story by Henry Van Dyke

I am standing upon the seashore. A ship at my side spreads her white sails to the morning breeze and starts for the blue ocean. She is an object of beauty and strength. I stand and watch her until at length she hangs like a speck of white cloud just where the sea and sky come to mingle with each other.

Then someone at my side says: "There, she is gone!"

"Gone where?"

Gone from my sight. That is all. She is just as large in mast and hull as she was when she left my side and she is just as able to bear her load of living freight to her destined port.

Her diminished size is in me, not in her. And just at the moment when someone at my side says, "There, she is gone!" there are other eyes watching her coming, and other voices ready to take up the glad shout. "Here she comes!"

And that is dying.

Death

Sent to RMS by Bob Nations; author unknown.

Death
   is
God carrying us
  in one of his
arms while the other
      f l i n g s aside
     heaven's
      door.

  Welcoming us
    back to the
blazing hearth
   of our first
    home.

And
  those inside, having
arrived long before
  us, rush to the
  door like glad
   children,
   shouting

They're
   here!
      They're here!

Death has a bad name
  on earth, but in
  heaven it is a house-

warming party
everytime the
door opens.

And God does
not forget his earth-
bound children, sad &
left behind. He leaves
the party early
to enter into
their despair
with them.

And to get
them ready
for their own
parties. . . .

Someday.

14. Divorce Changes
Interview with Ken Burkel by RMS

Ken was separated. He and his estranged spouse shared parenting of their two teenage sons, alternately being the primary parent. However, she decided she wanted her share of the equity in their house, to go on with her life. He was living in the home they had bought and lived in together while married. So Ken called a local real estate firm and got two appraisals. Both agents were eager to represent him as sales agent and gave him exaggerated values and promises as to how much his house would sell for if they marketed it. He didn't want to move, but felt he had no other choice to raise the money to pay his estranged wife her share of equity in the house.

A person he knew through training at his former employer's business learned he was separated and was thinking of selling his home because of the divorce. Her husband, Roy, was also a realtor and was leading support groups for recently separated or divorced persons at his church. She told Roy about Ken. He sent Ken a marketing letter regarding his home. Then he followed up with a phone call and got an appointment to meet Ken and look at his house. Ken reluctantly agreed to have Roy come by his home to look at his house and possibly list it. He felt "burned" by the first two agents who were so anxious and ready to sell his home, because he really didn't want to move. However, all he owned was about $6,000 and the equity in the house, so he felt trapped and unable to solve his problem.

Roy showed up, carrying a pocket dictaphone. As they walked through the house, Roy would make notes to himself about room size and details of the property. At the same time he was maintaining an ongoing series of questions about Ken and his particular situation and why he was wanting to sell, etc. Later, Ken realized his guard came down as Roy seemed genuinely interested in him and his life and needs and wants, while also being very professional about recording details related to the property. So he shared why he was interested in selling his house. Roy asked him if he wanted to sell. Ken answered no, he really didn't want to sell, but he didn't know how to get the money to pay his wife's share of the equity.

Before Roy left, he encouraged Ken not to sell, but to find a way to stay in the house for the time being. Since so much in Ken's life was changing with the divorce, Roy suggested staying in the home would be better for him and his sons. Ken was shocked and surprised that Roy encouraged him not to sell since that was his livelihood! Roy said he could sell a couple years down the road. In addition, as Roy left the house, he mentioned he led a support group for recently separated and divorced persons. It was late spring. The group was both closed and full (had maximum numbers for cohesiveness and sharing) since it had been meeting weekly for many months. It met for about nine months, and was almost completed. Therefore, new people were assigned to a fall schedule. Roy told him he could join a new group in the fall when a new group would be formed. Ken felt hurt and rejected, not understanding why he couldn't participate immediately (aren't churches supposed to be open?). However, he did end up joining the new group in the fall. (Later, he came to understand the "closed group" concept and its purpose to build deep trust, confidentiality, and openness among members. Cohesiveness and intimacy increases in closed groups. This is essential for promoting the healing process. His new group became a significant influence and healing process in his life and career.)

After Roy left, Ken went inside and went to his office.

He sat down at his desk and began to weep and pray, asking God for guidance and help to figure out how to get the money. About an hour later, his phone rang. He had a call from a company on whom he had made a sales call some time previously. Usually his commissions on a sale averaged $800-1,200. However, he was told the company had a need for multiple offices to purchase his services/products, and the end result was that his commission was $27,000 on that sale! Very unusual. Enough to pay off his wife's equity in their home and enable him to stay in the home with his sons. Ken says he believes there are miracles all the time, but many times people do not notice or pay attention. To him, this was a miracle!

Some years later, he was a pallbearer for Roy's funeral. While sitting in the service, as an emotional eulogy was shared, he found himself thinking of Roy — he called him his "guardian angel" — and praying that Roy would continue to guide his life. He felt a tugging on his jacket. It happened again; the feeling was so intense and distinct, that he turned around to see who was tugging on his jacket behind him. No one was sitting behind him. At that moment he decided the tug was his guardian angel (Roy present in spirit), assuring him that his prayer was answered. Another one of those little miracles.

In Ken's case, when he joined a recently separated and divorced support group in the fall, he met another participant who became his partner in a new venture. Today, years later, they have established a very successful entrepreneurial company offering telecommunication auditing and consulting services to businesses that continues to grow and expand as the industry changes. So the ending of his marriage became a doorway to a whole new life and business. Out of the depths of his pain and loss, he developed new personal friendships and a whole new career direction. Grace disguised and wrapped up in grief. Sometimes people miss the gift because of the dark package in which it arrives. However, Ken did not miss the Grace. Ken and one of his business partners have chosen to share the Grace by leading support groups for recently separated and divorced people through their church community. A wonderful example of Paying It Forward!

The most powerful weapon on earth is the human soul on fire.
— Marshall Foch

15. Job Loss
From a source in Winston-Salem, NC

While driving to Fred's wife's relative's funeral a few hours distant, his car phone rang. As he answered it, he heard his boss's voice. When the boss heard where he was going, he said he'd call him later, after the funeral.

A couple hours later he was driving toward Durham on the interstate, to keep his day's sales appointments when the phone rang again. He answered, figuring it would be his boss. His wife was already on her way back to their home in her car. In amazement and shock, Fred heard his boss instruct him to return home without keeping his appointments. There had been a reorganization of the company the night before and his job had been eliminated. No preparation. No concern for his safety while driving on a busy superhighway. He was directed to call and cancel his sales appointments.

Eventually the company completely folded, and today it no longer exists, but Fred has never forgotten the stunning blow of that cold, irresponsible-for-human-welfare phone call. It took eight months of intense effort — full time — to land a new job. The higher the salary and position, the longer the delay in finding a new job, is the norm.

One of the coping skills Fred employed was to join a group of job-seekers who met weekly. Here he found both support for the terrible roller coaster of emotions connected to job loss and comfort and acceptance by peers, and the opportunity to learn new skills related to marketing himself and how to network to find a job. The leader of the job loss support group, who had been leading groups for persons unemployed and seeking employment for fourteen years, conducted not only the weekly one hour meetings, but also a twenty-hour workshop on the classic book *What Color Is Your Parachute?* He had been trained in the tools and skills of the book by the author in a prior year. Intense, exhaustive self-analysis of strengths, weaknesses, experiences, abilities, achievements, and dreams helped participants, including Fred, discover who they are in the present, so that they can focus their assets for job-hunting in the current job arena. It also taught them how to market themselves and present themselves and network to find the best jobs by becoming an "insider" in a company in which they seek employment.

It took eight months for Fred, through the new coping skills he learned in both weekly meetings and the workshop, to choose a company of interest to him and to get a job offer from them. In the months of no job, he sought out and applied for many jobs, not quitting even when turned down. Continuing to network and build relationships within the firm he had selected to pursue allowed him to eventually find the job he finally landed. Now he can look back and laugh about his journey from being fired in such a shocking manner to developing new strengths and coping skills and his ability to land with his feet on solid ground, and achieve finding a new desirable position.

★ ★ ★ ★ ★ ★ ★

I met Fred at a support group meeting after he had landed his new job. He was already past the months of anguish and cycles of emotions so common among those who deal with job loss. He presented a positive, upbeat attitude and was encouraging others who had just lost jobs and were in fear or despair to have hope — he had been where they were and knew their pain, but they could also come through, a better person and with another job. But in the midst of the fire, it sometimes is difficult to hang on to hope and self-confidence. A support group such as

Professionals in Transition₍ᵣ₎ is key to surviving this crisis.

Loss of a job in a culture that often bases one's identity on one's career position is a very difficult thing, both for the man/woman who loses the job and for the family. Emotions run wide and deep, from intense fear to anxiety to anger to great grief to deep shame to shock and disbelief. Many hide the loss from the outside world — if possible. The family's lifestyle has to change due to economic changes, so they experience loss as well. Often a new job requires relocation, with loss of the social networks and support systems at all levels within the family: church, school, neighborhood, social organizations, and business colleagues. A person who loses his job must create energy and a positive attitude to pursue new endeavors, while also grieving the losses. He has to believe in himself and his talents and abilities and be able to communicate and articulate them for new roles and positions, as well as handle the incredible (normal) emotional roller coaster ride of pursuing new work, promoting oneself, constantly being under a spotlight in job interviews, maintaining hope in the future and faith in himself and waiting. Waiting is very wearing for all concerned. Sometimes families have to declare bankruptcy, if finances are greatly disrupted.

Sometimes the person who lost a job is secretly glad — because she didn't like her work or boss. (Personality clashes which lead to firing or resignation are not unusual — fifty percent or more people will experience this sometime or another in their lifetimes.) However, her spouse and/or children may be angry at her because of how it disrupts their lives. Sometimes, as industries change, jobs are no longer needed and a person must develop new skills or a whole new career. All of this requires enormous coping skills and deep self-assessment.

Emotions run high for all involved. One friend shared how she and her husband left academia and moved to a new location. He took a job in a business and was very happy. She, on the other hand, was very unhappy as a new young mother with no career. At night, to cope, she would get in the car and drive for hours to think, while her husband slept soundly. To this day, he never realized her terrible depression and how she coped. Eventually she returned to school for an advanced degree, which opened new doors of challenge for her and also created new social networks.

Job loss is a major crisis in our American way of life. And therefore, we need new social networks and tools to assist people who are facing such a crisis. People need support and encouragement and assistance to ride the roller coaster and emotions of job loss and searching and struggles to hang on to self-esteem and confidence and hope! See story #16, pp. 72-73, for resources on job loss.

Never give up, for that is just the place and time that the tide will turn.

— Harriet Beecher Stowe

16. Job Loss Creates a Bridge for Others
From an interview with Damian Birkel

It was a cold, rainy, stormy Friday in Cleveland, Ohio, in the 1980s. Damian was looking forward to leaving the office and going on vacation with his wife Donna and new baby. At twenty-seven years old, he was already successful as a buyer, with an "outstanding" rating. However, shortly before six o'clock that evening, his new boss told him to come to his office. The garage closed at six and so Damian wondered if it couldn't wait. The boss said no. Damian said he needed to get his car out of the garage before it closed. The boss told him to get it out, park on the street (and the boss would pay), and return to his office. Amazed, curious, and irritated all at once, Damian did as asked, and returned to the office soaked from the storm. Inwardly, he wondered what was so important on Friday at 6:00 PM before a vacation!

He had no clue—until his boss told him he was "unsatisfactory," and "there is nothing you can do" and "think about it while you're on vacation." He was given notice, though expected to return to work, knowing that in ninety days he would be without a job. Damian felt "literally blown away."

He continued to do his job, while simultaneously trying to find new employment. He felt too ashamed, too humiliated to tell anyone. And he was very angry. During those three months, he felt he was a loser, confused and disoriented. To make matters worse, he had responsibility for a new house and a new baby. It felt like his life was over. No wonder: Job loss, according to a *Fortune* magazine report, is one of the top ten most stressful events in life.

Later, Damian recognized that his job loss resulted from

a personality conflict, which almost everyone will experience at least once during his or her career lifetime. Oil and water will not mix!

During his ninety days of "probation," although no one at the time realized that he was technically "fired," his wife was a major support. She told him, "You'll come out on the other side." He also leaned on God to get him through. He had experienced a tough time at age eighteen when his father died, so he was familiar with the feelings of grief. A face-saving action was to request that his brother-in-law allow him to use part of his office. He told his colleagues that he created a new job for himself, saying he was going into advertising specialties.

After receiving seven promotions in seven years, many realized that Damian's departure story was a graceful way to leave an awkward situation. Most avoided him, but a job interview opportunity came to him "out of the blue,' when a sales representative called to let him know that his rival had just resigned from the competitor. The sales rep had always presented his products to Damian with integrity, honesty and respect, and never forgot Damian's kindness. Damian interviewed for the position and got the job! As a result, he traveled the world developing new and exciting products that appeared in department stores across the world.

The lesson is never to burn your bridges with people or an old job—you never know what may unfold in the future.

Then in 1987, Damian relocated from Cleveland, his lifelong residence, with his wife and two young children, ages seven and three, to accept a prestigious marketing/ merchandising position at a Fortune Fifty corporation in North Carolina. He purchased a new home, based on his generous new salary. Soon, ninety-eight percent of the company's employees were given walking papers, though eventually all of the support personnel and the majority of the upper management were placed into other divisions. Middle managers were wiped out and sent to an outplacement firm. In his short time in his new location, he had traveled for business and worked overtime, thus limiting his connections and support within his new community. All he had was his family to help in dealing with the shock, grief, guilt, bewilderment, shame, and anger of yet another lost career, job, and identity.

In his struggle to pick up the pieces of his life, feeling like a ship lost at sea, Damian wondered what organization might be available to help him recover emotionally and make connections for a new position. However, he did not find such help. Almost eight months later, his agonizing job search ended when he assumed a new position as a product marketing manager within a different division of the same corporation.

His experience and painful journey had created a seed of an idea: If there were no organizations available to help those between jobs, why not start one? A year later, over lunch, he and a former colleague commiserated over the trauma of job searching and trying to penetrate the professional network of a small town. Damian shared his idea of creating a job support group, and his friend was solidly encouraging. The friend introduced him to his career counselor. The team explored the concept and out of that conversation emerged two major goals: 1) to create "safe space" where people could discuss the multiple issues of the reemployment process, and 2) to provide each other with information, job leads, perspective, hope, and the best possible chance for reemployment.

His friend persuaded the local Red Cross chapter to donate space for meetings. They passed out fliers anywhere that people were congregating, and Damian ran an ad in the calendar sections of the local newspapers. And so, out of the shock and trauma of two job losses and three company reorganizations, Damian created a new non-profit organization: Professionals in Transition®, Support Group, Inc. The organization has served over 1,500 members and their families without charge since 1992 and has become a permanent resource in the community. He left his job in 1999 to become the Executive Director and Founder of this valuable and viable nonprofit organization. He is the author of three books including *Career Bounce-Back!*, *Surfing the Emotional Wave* (CBB Books), and an accompanying videotape series. He also serves as the webmaster for the Professionals in Training® website, www.jobsearching.org.

He also consulted with his former professor and longtime friend John P. Wilson, Ph.D., a national authority on post-traumatic stress disorder. Dr. Wilson encouraged him to contact one of his former colleagues, Dr. Elisabeth Kubler-Ross, the psychiatrist who had blazed a trail in studies on death and dying. Dr. Kubler-Ross graciously invited him to meet her at her Virginia home to talk about his ideas on the connection between death and dying and job loss. She agreed that her theories could be applied to job loss: "A loss is a loss is a loss. It doesn't make any difference whether it's job loss or a death in the family." So Damian adopted the grieving process to his "bounce-back" program. Another significant influence upon his program was Richard Nelson Bolles' book, *What Color is Your Parachute?*

As Damian's organizational content and structure evolved, he integrated the job loss and recovery grief process with job skills development. Meetings employed concepts from his experiences with Al-Anon, which he attended in connection with a family member's needs. The format developed over time into a three-part structure: First, the information exchange (for general announcements, job opportunity presentations, and updates from PIT alumni. When someone landed a new job, they created a celebration with food and a certificate.) Second, members introduced themselves, and took turns sharing their job-hunting experiences and recounting the emotional weather of the previous week. Third, during the less structured "fellowship-exchange," members and alumni offered one another job leads, feedback, and advice. Establishing the organization as a grass-roots, volunteer-led support group, Damian educated himself in the entire reemployment process and sought to cover bases omitted by other job support resources. He discovered that job loss had no socially acceptable way of working through grief, and he determined to add that information and support to his program.

PIT® revolves around the concepts of "heal your soul first, then seek a job," and "help others as you would like to be helped, and you will be helped." Adapting Dr. Kubler-Ross's Grieving Process to the Emotional Wave of Unemployment (the Emotional-Wave™ or E-Wave™ for short in the *Career Bounce-Back!* series) helps the jobless come to terms with and understand the six stages: Shock and Denial, Fear and Panic, Anger, Bargaining, Depression, and Temporary Acceptance. Intellectual awareness allows some reclaiming of control over one's life, and helps interrupt the cycle of drowning hopelessness.

Damian also addresses the Family-Wave™ or F-Wave™. The f-wave parallels the e-wave in terms of its stages, yet it does not follow the same sequence or pace for family members. And this is not a lateral, sequential process, but cyclical and uneven in its process. Family members often have deep feelings of powerlessness and helplessness as they deal with the changes that result from a family member becoming unemployed. PIT's advice is: "Unemployment is a temporary condition."

The journey to where Damian and PIT are today has been a major testing time. Holding down a sixty-hour job, for eight years he has also spent forty hours a week on his dream to create a self-sustaining professionals-in-transition support group. He told how one day he went to Mass, and in deep anguish prayed, "I'm tired of doing this alone, and I'll never forget what it's like to be unemployed." Apparently God heard his passionate plea, because things began to improve. Several corporations and foundations have provided financing to help with the work. Damian continues to seek ways to reach out, spread the word, and grow the services of the organization to meet needs. Damian is now working in PIT full time as Executive Director. Hundreds of graduates honor him for his passion, commitment, dedication, vision, and leadership in helping them survive and thrive out of the Dark Night of Job Loss.

17. A Change in Business: Making Lemonade from Lemons

From an interview with Jimmy and Roger Nichols

As in many areas of the United States, North Carolina in the late nineties and turn of the century has been facing and experiencing massive changes as we move from the Agricultural Age to the Industrial Age through the Service Age and into the Information Age. North Carolina has seen thousands of jobs lost in industries like textiles, furniture, tobacco, and banking. Some went overseas; some just disappeared. The economy of North Carolina has reeled from the switch from the Age of Manpower to the Age of Mindpower, where you are no longer rewarded for the hours you put in but instead for what you put into those hours. In the recent recession, North Carolina faced unemployment rates among the highest in the nation. Many people, often with little warning or time to prepare, discovered there was no such thing as a "secure job in a secure company."

One industry in North Carolina with a time honored history of over 150 years, since it began in the 1850s, was the tobacco warehousing business. Tobacco has been one of the major farm crops in the South for hundreds of years, and over time the need for the services of a middleman developed to meet the needs of farmers who grew the tobacco and the companies who purchased the tobacco and manufactured it into various products.

Roger Nichols, age sixty-five today, worked his whole life in the tobacco industry, first as a farmer (like his father before him), raising tobacco to sell, and later as the owner and operator of tobacco warehouses. He lived on a farm in Surry County (Andy Griffith Country!) and taught his four sons the business. Jimmy, his third born son, age thirty-six as I write this, went to college for a few short weeks, but dropped out to join his father in the farming business. His older brother Gary was tragically killed in an automobile accident at age twenty-one almost twenty-five years ago. Roger says he felt he would die with grief. His father took him by the arm at the funeral and told him, "You still have three sons to raise. They need you." So he managed to go on with his life, focusing on what he still had instead of what he had lost. But his sadness over his loss comes across in his tone and eyes as he speaks of those days of grief. A loss so deep is never forgotten; one only learns to live with it.

Roger's second son, Tim, age forty-one, had asthma as a child, so he never became an active member of the family business. Instead he publishes a popular magazine called *Domicile* and works as an interior designer. The youngest son, Sam, age thirty-one, also became active in the family business, bypassing college.

Father and sons owned a warehouse in Mount Airy, and then five years ago they bought a second warehouse in Winston-Salem, and in 1991 and 1996 two more warehouses in Shelbyville, Kentucky. Roger always liked his property to be well-maintained, so he invested in his business by borrowing heavily from banks for improvements.

North Carolina farmers raise flue cured tobacco, while Kentucky farmers raise burley tobacco. As tobacco warehousers, Roger and his sons would hold auctions for the farmers to sell their crops to the manufacturing companies, in North Carolina between August and November and in Kentucky from Thanksgiving week until February. Their volume of sales was around ten million pounds of flue cured and ten million pounds of burley tobacco. In the "off season" (no auctions), the Nichols would meet with farmers and the companies to sell their services and build relationships.

Three years ago, the tobacco companies (Phillip Morris, R. J. Reynolds, and others) started to contract directly with the farmers to save money. And then two years ago (in 2000) they directly contracted about ten percent of the tobacco crops. A year later, in 2001, the direct contracting increased to eighty-five percent of the crops. This action by the companies essentially eliminated the middleman, such as the Nicholses, cutting them out of the tobacco warehouse business.

Roger shared with me his thinking and feelings in that two- to three-year period. He said he never saw the train of change coming. When it rounded the bend in the first year (when a Pilot Program began), he kept thinking that contracting directly between farmer and company would not succeed. "No way!" he said to himself. Even after ten percent of their business disappeared, he thought the concept would fail. He recognizes now that he was in denial — the first step in the grief process. He calls it "wishful thinking." He hoped the new deals would fail. After all, he had built his whole life around the warehouse business; he had gone heavily into debt buying and fixing up warehouses in three cities, and had spent forty years building relationships with his farmer customers and company customers! He had always worked to provide quality services and maintain excellent working rapport and trust. They had purchased and fixed up a home in Kentucky where they stayed during the months of doing business with those farmers. It was like "being fired" from his own company, he said. He felt deep sadness at the loss of his business because he had no control over the changes.

Last year, with eighty-five percent of their business gone, and facing a deep recession in North Carolina, the shock hit him hard. Both Kentucky and North Carolina markets were affected, as land allotments for growing tobacco were also cut. In 2001, the Nichols' volume dropped to two and one-half million pounds, and they did not even go to Kentucky at all. In 2002, their volume was zero percent! Gone!

A whole business had disappeared. They could have filed bankruptcy, but decided instead to try to work with the banks, their creditors, to pay off their debts. At this writing, they have been able to avoid bankruptcy, but their buildings will need to be sold or remodeled to accommodate another type of business.

★   ★   ★   ★   ★   ★   ★

In 1998, to supplement the family tobacco warehouse business, another focus had been started to add income. The Nicholses began buying and selling parcels of land. However, as the tobacco warehousing business evaporated in 2001, they devoted all their time to the land business and started the Nichols Land Company. Besides land, they began to purchase, renovate, and resell houses, from Wilmington to Hickory/Lenoir to Virginia to Blowing Rock. The recession, however, "threw them for a loop." The banks refused to loan them more money for their new land and housing business. Fortunately, because of their solid relationships and good reputation for integrity in the community (and maybe "because they felt sorry for us"), local individuals began to loan them money to operate the new business. Private investors could profit from loaning them money when interest rates in traditional institutions were very low because the Nicholses paid them higher interest rates.

Roger had always felt tobacco was a "sure shot"; he "knew it like the back of his hand." The land company, he felt, was a gamble. The Nicholses, nonetheless, had always been competitive and they "liked a challenge," so they decided to throw their skills into the new venture. In 2001 they bought and sold thirty-five houses. They were able to sell thirty in the first four months of the next year and set a goal of at least one hundred. At some future point they would like to sell two hundred a year.

As middlemen in tobacco, they knew how to buy and sell for a profit, how to deal with people and keep all parties satisfied, and how to make deals, and they had excellent people skills. So they decided to "keep on keeping on"; their philosophy was: "We can't give up!"

Roger's wife kept the books for the warehouses, and retired five years ago. She was very supportive during the transition. Jimmy's wife is a nurse and works in a pediatric doctor's office. They have three children. Sam has a wife, two stepsons, and a daughter. His wife runs their office.

Last year was a very difficult year. During tough times the brothers get a boost from a calendar of "Stress Busters" featuring inspirational quotes. Jimmy especially likes one that reads: "Many of life's failures are people who did not realize how close they were to success when they gave up," (Thomas Edison), and another, anonymous, one that says "It's often not a matter of trying harder but of trying differently. Before giving up completely on something that's important to you, consider another approach."

In the early stages of the land company, when they were having difficulty borrowing money, they started a mortgage company so they could loan money to purchasers of their homes. They wanted to spur quicker response by prospective buyers and offer a full service company. They proceeded to get the bonding and a license and to go through the Banking Commission to meet requirements to create a mortgage company. At this writing they were close to being able to operate as a mortgage company.

They began the land company in a horse barn, which they used for one year as an office. From these humble beginnings, they grew into a nicely renovated home in Mount Airy where they can meet customers and operate their land company. Their story is one of courage and commitment, an inspiration for anyone who dreams of creating a successful business. They have goals and dreams. Even Roger, at age sixty-five — not ready to retire — spoke of his dream that someday their little renovated house-into-office would become an office high rise! Jimmy wants to "build this company." Together, the three (Roger, Jimmy, and Sam) work as a team to create ideas and implement them. They also seek good people for key positions, people with experience and integrity. Roger's Quaker faith has been a strong foundation for getting him through the rough spots and road blocks, and for his commitment to treating employees, customers, and suppliers with integrity.

The Nicholses represent the heart and soul of the family entrepreneurial business in America, which finds a way to rise out of the ashes as did pioneers of yesteryear who founded this country and tamed the land for cultivation. The Nichols' courage, creativity, and determination in overcoming great difficulties serves as an inspiration for all of us.

———————————

Things work out for the best for those who make the best of the way things work out.

— Author unknown

The Comfort Zone
From Voice Mail by Women on Fire Support Group

I used to have a comfort zone
Where I thought I could not fail.
Same four walls and busy work
Were really more like jail.
I longed so much to do the things
I'd never done before.
But I've stayed inside my comfort zone
And paced the same old floor.
I said it didn't matter
That I wasn't doing much.
I said I didn't care for things
Like diamonds, furs, or such.
I claimed to be so busy
With the things inside my zone.
But deep inside I longed
For something special of my own.
I could not let my life go by
By watching others win.
I held my breath
And stepped outside
And let the change begin.
I took a step with new strength
I'd never felt before.
I kissed my comfort zone goodbye
And closed and locked the door.
If you are in a comfort zone
Afraid to venture out.
Remember that all winners
Were at one time filled with doubt.
A step or two,

And words of praise
Can make your dreams come true.
Greet your future
With a smile.
Success is there for you!

— Anonymous

18. Two Choices
From an email; author unknown

Michael is the kind of guy you love to hate. He is ever in a good mood and always has something positive to say. When someone asks him how he is doing, he replies, "If I were any better, I would be twins!" As a supervisor, he is a natural motivator. If an employee is having a bad day, Michael is right there, telling the employee how to look on the positive side of the situation.

Seeing this style really made me curious, so one day I went up to Michael and asked him, "I don't get it! You can't be a positive person all of the time. How do you do it?" Michael replied, "Each morning I wake up and say to myself, you have two choices today. You can choose to be in a good mood or you can choose to be in a bad mood. I choose to be in a good mood. Each time something bad happens, I can choose to be a victim or choose to learn from it. I choose to learn from it. Every time someone comes to me complaining, I can choose to accept their complaining or I can point out the positive side of life."

"It's not that easy," I protested.

"Yes, it is," Michael said. "Life is all about choices. When you cut away all the junk, every situation is a choice. You choose how you react to situations. You choose how people affect your mood. The bottom line is: It's your choice how you live your life."

Soon thereafter, I left the Tower Industry to start my own business. We lost touch, but I often thought about Michael when I made a choice about life instead of reacting negatively to a setback. Several years later, I heard that Michael was involved in a serious accident; he had fallen some sixty feet from a communications tower. After eighteen hours of surgery and weeks of intensive care, Michael was released from the hospital with rods placed in his back.

I saw Michael about six months after the accident. When I asked him how he was, he replied, "If I were any better, I'd be twins. Wanna see my scars?" I declined to see his wounds, but I did ask him what had gone through his mind as the accident took place.

"The first thing that went through my mind was the well-being of my soon-to-be-born daughter," Michael replied. "Then, as I lay on the ground, I remembered that I had two choices: I could choose to live or I could choose to die. I chose to live."

"Weren't you scared? Did you lose consciousness?" I asked.

Michael continued, "The paramedics were great. They kept telling me I was going to be fine. But when they wheeled me into the ER and I saw the expressions on the faces of the doctors and nurses, I got really scared. In their eyes, I read 'He's a dead man.' I knew I needed to take action."

"What did you do?" I asked.

"Well, there was a big burly nurse shouting questions at me," said Michael. "She asked if I was allergic to anything. 'Yes, I replied.' The doctors and nurses stopped working as they waited for my reply. I took a deep breath and yelled, 'Gravity.' Over their laughter, I told them, 'I am choosing to *live*. Operate on me as if I am alive, not dead.'"

Michael lived, thanks to the skill of his doctors, but also because of his amazing attitude that we all have the choice to live every day fully. Attitude is everything.

———————

Therefore do not worry about tomorrow, for tomorrow will worry about its own things. Sufficient for the day is its own trouble.

— Matthew 6:34

19. Losing One's Soul Mate Partner
From an interview with a widow

Linda describes herself as "an eagle," someone who has always been upbeat and happy. After a period of loss, she states, "My Spirit is beginning to soar like an eagle. Today I am very happy; however, when my husband John was living, I was supremely happy. I do not expect to feel that way again this side of eternity."

Linda explains that her heart hurt, literally, for three years after her husband's death, which came one night very suddenly. "It is true: people do have a broken heart, which needs healing," she says. They had been married and soul mates for over forty years. A strong and positive woman by nature, she found that naming her grief process, her many feelings and stages, aloud to caring friends enabled her to bear the pain of her acute loss. In addition, she had help from a pastor, who specialized in grief counseling. Without his support, she believes, she would not have come through this deep valley to the mountaintop. "God worked through him," she assures me.

Born and raised in a small midwestern city, Linda and John met in grade school. He had decided early on he would marry her. So they shared a long history and bond together as school classmates and friends. Eventually they married and raised a family. She remained a homemaker while he became the bread earner and built a successful business. Their life together was good: They had various leadership roles in both civic and church circles and rich friendships as their children grew up and also married. Linda describes her husband as a loving and caring person, husband, father, grandfather, and community, church, and business leader. He was known, respected, and loved within their community by many people. After his death, so many of these people shared their love for him with her; this added value to her life as she learned how he had helped others. She believes what he gave to others has come back to her: "The circle of love is unending." So she believes she has "reaped the fruit" of her husband's love from the seeds he planted and nurtured. She has discovered that "people we lose live on in the hearts and memories and stories of others." Linda was grateful for these verbal gifts of loving memory. She accepted them as God's work in her life to heal her heart.

Linda has been amazing in her journey through grief. She deliberately chose to face the demons of widowhood by entering consciously into the depths of pain, despair, depression, anguish, and stages of grief to find healing. In so doing she found the strength and creativity to create a new life alone. Her strong, active faith was her bridge to surviving, and even thriving, as a widow who wanted to be "more than conqueror."

One time a very close friend called just to say "Good morning." She wanted to drive by and pop in for a quick visit to seek Linda's advice. She invited Linda to go shopping with her. Then she observed: "You're hurting, aren't you?" Her perceptive kindness gave Linda the wonderful opportunity to have a desperately needed good cry with a loving and caring person.

Linda and John both were profoundly committed to their Christian faith in life. Linda faced the greatest loss in her life when her husband died suddenly with a massive heart attack. However, her deep, abiding faith in a loving God sustained her. This deep faith also brought some intense testing, because some did not understand her spiritual anchor.

After John's death, as so frequently occurs in the grief process, Linda was unable to sleep. She was not one to use drugs under normal circumstances. Nonetheless, her worried family insisted she get a prescription from her doctor. When she still wasn't sleeping, she was given a second, and then a third different medication over a short span of time. After the third prescription, all the medications took effect together (probably potentiating each other). Often older persons can become confused and disoriented from medications. This is also not uncommon in grieving persons. Her doctor did not realize at the time the potentiation of the three different drugs. Her children, concerned at her apparent mental status and decompensation, took her to the doctor's office; she ended up being committed to a psychiatric hospital.

However, previous to her hospitalization, within ten days of John's death, she had attended several business meetings and spoken to the entire company concerning the future of the company; she assured them that "everything would go on and the company would be maintained as it was when John was alive." She was functioning appropriately. Her children were scared because they learned from her friends that she was not sleeping and would be up working on business matters and paperwork in John's home office. John had prepared her for his possible death by his advanced planning and educating her about his business, and she knew what was expected of her, because they had gone over things together frequently. Because Linda and John were so close, the children feared for her welfare without him, thinking she was losing her mental ability. She simply was grieving deeply and using the time at night when she could not sleep to focus on plans John had prepared ahead of time.

(In our traditional medicine oriented culture, so many people think a pill is the answer to any problem. I will never forget my own experience as a student nurse caring for an Italian gentleman who had a bowel obstruction and refused surgery. After his death, the family met in his room and their cries and weeping could be heard all over the hospital unit. The head nurse called the doctor in charge and obtained an order for a sedative for the family. After taking graduate level courses and studying the grief process in psychiatric-mental health nursing, I realized that they simply needed loving support and listening / acknowledging their pain and loss at that time. Their grief was normal and healthy, even if it was loud and emotional, which was an expression of their culture. It was the staff, however, who found the pain too terrible to bear and witness. It takes compassion, care, and a willingness to be with people in their anguish, even in acute, terrible losses and hurts. A pill is easier to provide, but much less effective because while it dulls the pain, it also prolongs the grief process.)

Linda later told a friend that if her family had found someone to stay with her in her own home at night—someone to provide listening and be with her during that acute crisis period—she would have been fine. She definitely was not mentally ill, though she experienced some confusion. Her family also did not realize how deep was her profound faith, which caused her to appear so labile: one moment weeping and grieving deeply, and the next rejoicing in her knowledge that John had gone home to be with God. Both feelings were real and genuine — and healthy. Unless people have received in advance education about grief and how to help people process and respond to their feelings, medication seems the appropriate intervention.

(While caring for my husband, I had had very little sleep for several months before my husband died from cancer. For many months after his death, I did not sleep except an hour or two a night. I would fall asleep and then abruptly awaken after one to two hours, and could not go back to sleep. So I would read. I was borrowing five to seven books on grief every week from the local hospice library, and reading them at night. I had a physical about a month after

Roy died and my doctor recommended three things: walk for an hour a day in the sunshine, take my estrogen, and vitamin E to protect my heart. She also gave me a prescription for a sleeping medication. I checked it in the *Physician's Desk Reference* and saw it could become addictive. So I decided to take it for about ten to fourteen days (to increase my sleep to four to five hours a night), and then switched to Valarian, a calming herb that Shaklee had recently put on the market; this I knew would be safer long term than the prescription. Gradually, over many months, I was able to increase my sleep hours from one or two to five consistently. After setting up AirSource, a new technological air purifier, in my home, I found my sleep deepened and lengthened to six or seven hours a night.)

★　★　★　★　★　★　★

At the psychiatric hospital, Linda faced new challenges: naturally positive, she encouraged others in group therapy one moment, and the next moment found herself grieving John's death as she identified with someone speaking of their own grief and loss. The staff decided she was manic-depressive, diagnosing her symptoms of up/down joy and sadness as an illness, and not appreciating her deep Christian faith and usually optimistic outlook on life. Her doctor ordered drugs appropriate for someone with a manic depressive illness. The nurses made sure she swallowed them whenever they gave her pills. Their paradigm of Linda was a person with psychosis, and they treated her accordingly.

However, Linda claims, "What was meant for evil, God meant for good" (see Genesis 45: 4-8). Her assigned roommate, a Native American, had been praying for a Christian to share her space. The Native American woman would say, "Come on, Mamma, let's walk!" and together they paced the hall. Linda had always loved to dress up and "look her best," so she gave her family lists of clothing and makeup she needed. Because she discussed the Lord so much with her roommate and others, she was placed in the quiet room to "stop talking so much about the Lord."

During her private sessions with the psychiatrist, she spoke of her marriage to John and their deep faith in God and loving relationship. He listened to her respectfully. In the end, he changed the official diagnosis to "severe grief over death of husband and over-medication," since he realized she was not mentally deranged. But the experience made her very determined to face her pain and find peace and wholeness again.

Her sister visited her at the hospital and after seeing Linda, called her children and told them to get her off medications because she was becoming a zombie. She had never before "taken medication and our family tends to be highly sensitive to medications." So they listened. As she was leaving the hospital, the hospital staff recommended she have an MRI, probably concerned about a possible brain tumor. Linda decided to "take charge of her life." She refused the MRI. "I got a fighting spirit quickly," she remembers. This became a turning point.

Later, she decided to check her hospital record to read their perceptions. She did review her record, assuring the hospital staff she was not going to sue them. But she told her doctor, "Commitment to or putting me under lockup in a psychiatric hospital was the most cruel and heartless thing to do to someone who had just lost the love of her life!" She confesses that she still has flashbacks to that difficult time in the hospital.

What she really needed was to be off medications and have someone stay with her until her acute grief abated. The medications accentuated normal confusion and disorientation during her acute grief and sleeplessness. Her roaming the house at night hunting for missing papers was not abnormal for someone who was in the acute phase of deep grief and was also an achiever.

Linda's husband had had a chronic illness for years, controlled with medication, and she was accustomed to awakening at night to check on him. The night John died, she awoke at 2:00 A.M. and found him clammy and not coherent. He did tell her he "didn't feel real well." He had an irregular heartbeat. She had exercised regularly for years, and therefore had the needed strength to get him up and prop him when he fell over in the bed. She decided to call 911 for an ambulance to take him to the hospital. She called a family member who went to the hospital with her.

At the emergency room, she waited and prayed: "Lord, you know I love my husband and want him to stay. However, not my will but thine be done!" The moment she ended her prayer, releasing her husband to God's love and care, the door opened. The doctor came up to her and told her John had died. She went to John, and hugged his body and said her goodbyes, knowing in faith they would meet again someday.

She told her minister, "John and I didn't get to say our goodbyes, but it's all right because we were all loved up. Everything that could have been said and done had been said and done. God has been preparing us."

That year, for her birthday, she wanted a special gift. John searched out a store in a distant town that had what she wanted. Together they made a trip to the store. She found five leather-bound rare antique books that she liked and asked him to help her select one to purchase. He suggested she buy all five. This was a first in their marriage. She told him at that time, "You don't have to buy me any more birthday gifts as long as you live, 'cause you've done it all in this!" A little over a month later he was gone. Little did she know her words were prophetic, but not because of John's not choosing to give her birthday gifts.

★ ★ ★ ★ ★ ★ ★

A week before his death, John had come home and was changing clothes in the bedroom. She heard him call, "Come here—Listen!" A male vocalist was singing: "You are the wind beneath my wings!" He said to her: "That's you, Linda! You are my wind!" They discussed and talked about everything during that last week. She had always hated when he took her to his home office and reviewed plans and business affairs, not because she didn't want to know, but because she knew all too well why he did it. He also gave her a mandate, as they read scripture and prayed together, "You'll have to lead our little family." She responded: "Some chance of that happening. That's your job, and you are doing it beautifully!"

After his death, so many people remarked upon how they had seen and talked with John during the two weeks prior to his passing. She felt it was like John somehow knew and was saying his goodbyes. Or God had planned those days and contacts, creating synchronicity.

Linda knows her love with John was unique and special. She misses their pillow talks and all the ways he loved and cherished her and afforded her the opportunity to love and cherish him.

Once Linda felt her calling was to be a helpmate in all aspects to her husband. Today she has a new calling to help others grow in love and faith, through a counseling ministry. She feels God has been preparing her for this role all her life, through all her experiences, both happy and hurt-filled. She finds deep fulfillment and purpose in sharing her Christian wisdom and faith with others.

To cope with her loss, she tried many avenues. She joined a choir, started a Christian book club, involved herself in her political party, became even more active at her church in prayer ministry, and focused on maintaining, improving and beautifying her garden and house. This latter activity has given her joy and a sense of accomplishment and surrounds her with nature and beauty.

Linda endured physical heart pain for a long time after John's death. To release the immense pain experienced through the heart muscle, and the loneliness, she spent four months screaming, on a daily basis, in her car or in her house. (Years ago I attended a therapy conference in Atlanta. One of my friends who was a counselor participated in a breakout session on anger and scream therapy. He had retained great anger from childhood experiences and discovered the release available through Scream Therapy. I had a broken engagement over twenty years ago, and I remember releasing the pain and hurt by screaming into a pillow so the neighbors did not hear. The truth is, there is more room outside to release energy than storing or stuffing it in one's body. It is healthier to release stress and negative emotion and pain from the body. Having a good cry is another healthy way to release intense feelings. Linda has utilized regular exercise and a careful diet and nutritional supplements to maintain her health.)

Linda released John along with the pain of loneliness. Over time her heart pain ceased as well. She is grateful to God for what John and she were spared by his quick death. John would never have wanted to be incapacitated — that would have been death to him, she realizes, even if he had lived.

She has created a beautiful memorial garden with a bench, flowers, trees, and a gurgling fountain—The Living Water of Life—in memory of John and made a special memorial gift to their church in honor of John and their life together. Her goal today is to generate love, life, laughter, light and music in her life and home.

As painful as losing John has been, she is grateful for

how he prepared her to assume financial and leadership responsibilities for her life after his death. Since the average age of a woman who is widowed is fifty-eight, women need to prepare for being a widow and husbands need to help them and participate in sharing information.

Linda believes the woman needs to develop awareness that she is likely to live beyond her husband. She needs to know as much as possible about the home, personal, and business affairs. Linda believes this does not have to be a morbid thing—just accountability and loving care for the other. Preparations need to be talked about before death comes, either suddenly and unexpectedly as a thief in the night, or as the end of an illness, which can be all-consuming, and physically and emotionally exhausting.

Linda recommends women get prepared in these ways:
A) Letting him show you details and records and paper work.
B) Making sure you know where things are so if they're needed, you can put your hands on them.
C) Getting recommendations on key people to trust, help you, and pave the way with these individuals.
D) Accepting communication of his love and care for you when he helps you become familiar with the essentials.

Linda has developed a series of tips for people who need to deal with a newly widowed woman:
♥ Do attend a seminar on grief to learn about the process ahead of time and what to expect.
♥ Don't avoid the widow! Include her; speak to her.
♥ Don't be afraid to speak the deceased person's name and share stories about the person who died. A widow will value and treasure all stories and memories of her husband shared by others. Even if she weeps as you tell her stories, she will nonetheless treasure every mention of his life.

♥ Do not say to a widow: "Oh, you will marry again!" A widow may have to tell others: "Please do not say that to me again. I find it very painful and inappropriate!" Widows do not like hearing their beloved spouse spoken of as if he could be replaced like a garment.

Over seven years have passed since John's death. At the seventh anniversary month of his death, Linda became aware that once again she was supremely happy. Her experience was that this happiness was not the same as with John when he was alive. It's more like apples and pears — you can't compare. They are equally good, but different. "The Lord has filled my life with Himself and that which He has for me to do. I am about my Father's business."

————————

For your Maker is your husband. . . .

— Isaiah 54:5

Yet in all these things we are more than conquerors through Him who loved us. For I am persuaded that neither death nor life. . . shall be able to separate us from the love of God which is in Christ Jesus our Lord.

— Romans 8:37-39.

20. Coping with Chronic Illness, Lupus
From an interview with Sue Erdmann

In the late nineties, Sue developed pleurisy (fluid around her lungs) and pericarditis (fluid around her heart). Her whole body became inflamed and every joint ached. She had a constant fever. She had difficulty walking, sitting, sleeping, and eating. Never before in her life had she been in so much pain. She was very scared.

Her doctor searched and searched to discover what her problem was. He would call her at night and ask about her symptoms and situation. Eventually, he sent her to a rheumatologist for tests. In 1998, her diagnosis was lupus and treatment was prescribed. She didn't want to be on medication long term, so she decided she would take what he ordered, and find a way to get off it as soon as possible. She was on 60 mg. of Prednisone, an immuno-suppressant, as well as Imuran and Plaquenil, an anti-malaria medication.

Initially, the diagnosis shocked her. She went into denial. Then she began asking why. She couldn't stand not knowing, so she read everything she could find on lupus to educate herself and to cope. She felt enormous fear. She thought she would die, but she wanted to stay alive. She had a daughter and son whom she wanted to raise. At that time, her daughter was in eighth grade and her son in sixth. She went on the internet to continue researching. She found a "support" group, but because the participants were very negative, she eventually dropped out. Sue had always been a positive person; her mental decision was to keep on being positive, and surround herself with positive people. She continued to seek, read, and explore how to improve her health and well-being.

She took a test provided by Diane Petosky, an international speaker on nutrition who also consults with people who have severe health challenges. Sue learned there was "something going on in the immune system." So she increased the supplements she was using and followed a regimented program. It took her nine months to get back to feeling better. Mostly, she was "religious" about taking her vitamins and watching her diet to avoid increasing her symptoms of lupus. She discovered that anytime she "cheated" and used sugar or dairy products, she would swell up; her fingers, hands, knees, feet, and face ballooned to reveal her indiscretions. And she would feel, well...terrible. This is how she discovered that what we put into our body is so important!

By October 2000, Sue had weaned herself off of Prednisone, and she started to decrease the other medications. She went off the medications gradually, with her caring doctor's best wishes and guidance. He didn't want her to stay on them either. They both felt hopeful for her future. She made sure he knew what she was taking. One day she had walked into his office with her shopping bag of vitamins, put them on his desk and asked if he had any problems with what she was taking. Her first rheumatologist "was blown away....but he came around." Her current doctor looked at the bottles and said, "Oh, Shaklee! They are a fine company." He had no problem at all with her Shaklee program. However, he advised her for her safety not to take any Chinese herbal medicines that didn't have any clinical tests.

Sue's Shaklee Supplement Program for Lupus

Juicing is very important. Sue drinks at least sixteen ounces of fresh fruit and vegetable juice daily. She uses the Champion Juicer and follows the recipes in the book *The Juiceman's Power of Juicing*, by Jay Kordich.

It's important to stay away from the nightshade

vegetables (eggplant, potatoes, mushrooms). Some folks have trouble with tomatoes, although Sue has been able to handle them, but just doesn't eat them every day. The way to check if your body is affected: cut them out of your diet, and add them back one at a time to see how your body responds. Sue swelled when she ate eggplant, potato, and mushrooms. Be especially careful about Shiitake mushrooms and supplements that contain them.

It's also very important to watch all parts of your diet: Sue cut out sugar, red meats, processed foods, dairy products, and foods that contain chemicals or additives. She also decided to eat only organic fruits, vegetables, and juices. "This was hard, but very worth it," she reported.

The following supplements (Shaklee) are what she started on, and the dosages that worked for her. She had to adjust to find the right levels. She recommends that you add or subtract, depending on your body's needs. She followed this program for eleven months, then gradually cut back. She took only Shaklee nutritional supplements.

Caroto Max (beta carotene)	3-6 capsules daily (antioxidant)
Alfalfa	10-20 tablets daily, depending on inflammation (antioxidant)
Vitamin C (Sustained Release)	5500 mg. daily
Vitamin E Plus	1600 IU (antioxidant)
Formula I	3 capsules daily
B Complex	8 tablets daily
Garlic	6 tablets daily
Zinc	100 mg daily
EPA	12 capsules daily
Lecithin	9 capsules daily
Super Cal Mag	8 daily (1500-2000 mg. Daily)
Vita Lea	2-4 daily
GLA	6 daily
Optiflora Pre-biotic/Probiotic	1 tsp. and 1 pearl daily
Osteokinetics	3-6 capsules daily

Sue split these up into three bowls, to take three times throughout the day. She subsequently reduced her total intake to one bowl, half at breakfast, half in the afternoon with a protein shake for a snack.

Shaklee Soy Protein / Fiber Shake:
3 Tablespoons Vanilla or Creamy Cocoa Soy Protein with 1 Tablespoon Fiber Blend. Mix in 10-12 oz. of juice and add frozen banana pieces and berries, a couple ice cubes, and blend in a blender. Add to Shake if you really ache (muscles): Fitness or Physique

Paudi Arco Tea:
    loose tea from the Health Food Store
    4 cups of boiling water
    1 Tablespoon tea
Steep for 20 minutes in non-metal pot. Drink 3 cups daily. (Store rest in refrigerator for the next day.) Always drink tea with food. One can work up to higher levels.

Two major things to avoid are Echinacea and alfalfa sprouts.

Also very important for strengthening the Immune System of Body:
- ♥ Use Shaklee cleaners (nontoxic, organic formulas, safe for environment, too)
- ♥ Use Enfuselle skin care and Shaklee Personal Care products
- ♥ Drink lots of Best Water (Shaklee's purified water)

Instead of meat products for proteins, try tofu and soy products. Sue orders in quantity from North Farm Coop or Blooming Prairie Coop, and shops at Whole Foods in Madison, Wisconsin, or Health Hut.

Chamomile tea is very soothing, as well as peppermint ginger tea.

Besides nutritional support, Sue shared how important it was to keep a positive attitude. There were days when she wanted to crawl under the covers and give up. She said, "Don't!!" Just take the day slower and sit down and write down everything that is positive in your life. Design a personal motto. Sue says hers is, "My lupus is living with me...I am not living with it!" She eventually decided that "there was a reason that God chose me to have lupus:" it (along with Shaklee) came into her life as a Gift, so she would be inspired to help others, and that is what her mission now has become.

Sue also added that she had a wonderful support system in her family and friends. Her husband was going to school for his master's degree, and experienced a midlife crisis in the midst of her illness, so for a time that was an added stressor in their lives. The shock of that period eventually brought them to a place where their relationship became the best ever.

Her dear friend and sister, Julie, was a steady, fabulous support. So were the girls on her soccer team and their families, who brought in dinners to her family for a month when she was really sick.

As Sue was getting better, she visited a friend who had Sheltie puppies. One puppy formed a special bond with her, and she ended up taking the puppy home after it always crawled close to her and licked her and seemed especially affectionate with her. The puppy, whom her son named Calvin, became a special gift because it made her get up to care for him. Even when she was not feeling well, she had to take him outside for a walk. Her pastor said the dog was her "Angel Dog," because while she was caring for him she did not get sicker and had no "flare ups."

After two and a half years, her Sheltie puppy had seizures. The family learned that Calvin had a brain tumor, and eventually he died. Right up to his death Sue took care of him and loved him — as he had done for her when she was ill. In spite of being sad at his leaving her, she felt Calvin had been a special gift during a difficult stretch of her life.

Sue recommends avoiding stress and taking naps if

you are tired. She says it's important not to get overly tired because it takes a long time to recover from exhaustion.

Also, exercise is very important — even if only a walk around the block — to help relieve the stiffness and joint pain and to boost one's spirits. Sue wanted to be a part of a positive support group, but did not find any in her area.

Sue shared a number of her favorite books, resources, and tapes, as well as an essay written for a school project by her daughter.

Because of her desire to help others cope with this disease, I am including her personal information in the Resource Section for those with Lupus.

Turning Point Essay
Written by Sue Erdmann's daughter Katie Lynn, age 12

The turning point in my life so far was when my mom was diagnosed with Lupus. This is a disease where your immune system attacks itself. The disease can also go into remission, or flare up. There have been many happenings in my life that made me grow from a child into an adult, but when Lupus came into my life, it turned everything upside down.

Most of my mom's problems with Lupus started before she knew she had the disease. She developed allergic reactions to certain foods and became more and more tired as the days went on. She lost all the pep and enthusiasm she had once had. The problems continued for about a year and a half. She then went to a specialist. Between our doctor and the specialist they figured out she had the disease. Along with my mom, our whole family suffered. My dad was on his last year of his MBA program, but was gone every other weekend. That left my mom, my brother and me home on weekends. Since I'm the eldest child, I had to take on many of the responsibilities that my mom and dad had been handling. My grandparents would come over and help out every week, but my brother and I did a lot of the work around the house. We had to assume responsibilities we took for granted when our mom used to do them. Even the simplest task, such as sweeping the wooden floors, we now had to do! I felt as if I was playing the role of "Mom." If friends called, I had to stop and think if mom would need me at that time, if it was too much time to leave her alone or if I had something I needed to get done. Other kids could just say, "Hey mom, I'm going to so-and-so's house." For me it wasn't like that anymore. I had to do some growing up fast.

Being positive at all times was now a must at our home. We always had to try to keep a positive outlook on things. My mom had always been the one with the positive out-look; now it was our turn. She used to tell us constantly that "she loved us." As she got sicker, we were the ones telling her we loved her, and being her support system. It was hard for her also because the easiest jobs she used to do, she now had to rely on someone else to do. Mom looked fine on the outside, but on the inside she was crumbling. It is a very humbling experience to see a parent falling apart. They had always been there as a support system and teacher, and now you see them needing you more and more. It's sad to think that your parents are no longer in-vincible; bad things can and just might happen to them.

From this tragic incident I developed many awesome aspects of my personality. I learned to laugh all you can; it's the best medicine. Also, I learned to not take people and objects for granted. Someday you could lose them and it'll be too late to enjoy them. Another lesson I learned was to take one task at a time. If you don't you'll be over-whelmed. I've also learned that your family is your best support system. If you don't have a close knit family, you're really missing out. My family has grown closer because of my mom's disease. Besides learning I had a great family, I found out who my true friends were. The ones that stuck with me and gave me a shoulder to cry on are still with me to this day! My parent's friends were great too. They all took turns bringing meals for us, so my mom wouldn't have to cook. The last, and most important, thing I learned was about myself. I learned to love myself for who I was. You're going to be stuck with yourself for your whole life, so you might as well like yourself. Learn to do activities you really want to do and are good at. Try to achieve all you can while you're alive. Also, set realistic goals for yourself and try to accomplish one every day.

I turned from a child to an adult/older person, in a matter of months. I learned many valuable lessons. I learned to take on responsibilities without complaining. I also grew strong in the discovery of myself. I realized I was what I was and I should love myself for it. Another lesson I learned was to not take my parents for granted. They won't always be around to give advice and love. I found all of these things out through a disease, Lupus.

―――――――――

Things which matter most must never be at the mercy of things that matter least.

— Goethe

Expect trouble in your life, because it will catch up with you sooner or later. Nobody escapes it. Trouble does not mean you are stupid or bad or guilty of some wrongdoing; it simply means you are a member of the human race. Remember it is not what happens to you that counts, but how you handle it.

— Ann Landers, in a commencement address

Cancer is So Limited

It cannot cripple love
It cannot shatter hope
It cannot corrode faith
It cannot eat away peace
It cannot destory confidences
It cannot kill friendships
It cannot shut out memories

It cannot silence courage
It cannot invade the soul
It cannot reduce eternal life
It cannot quench the Spirit
It cannot lessen the power
of the Resurrection.

— Author unknown

21. Loss of Pet
From an interview with a seatmate on a flight

On a recent trip, while flying, I met a young woman age thirty who was a mother with two daughters and was married to a sheriff. She was also a career woman. When she discovered I was a nurse, she asked if I had ever had experience with pulmonary emboli. I told her yes, I knew what it was.

My flying companion Constance proceeded to tell me the following story. About five months previously she had a Siamese cat that she loved dearly. One day it ran away. It was gone for three weeks. She grieved over the cat being gone, running ads, sending out and posting notices, calling friends, looking on the roads and streets close to her neighborhood. Then one day, driving to work about three miles from her house, she saw a cat alongside of the road, dead. She stopped to check it out and discovered it was her pet cat. She called her husband and said she had to go to work, but asked if he would bury it when she got home that evening. However, when they went to pick it up, the cat was gone, probably retrieved by the animal catchers.

Constance started having severe chest pains. She thought she was having a heart attack. Tests were run, but her heart proved to be fine, and they discharged her. However, her doctor called back three or four days later. He asked her to come back in. After further testing, she was discovered to have multiple pulmonary emboli (clots in her lungs) and was hospitalized. Later, she discovered she had almost died. She wondered if her grief over her lost — then dead — cat had caused it. Her doctor said no, it hadn't.

Soon after her hospitalization, her younger brother, a

student going to college full time and also working full time, was under a lot of pressure. He was admitted to the hospital in another city. She went to see him. He also had pulmonary emboli. Constance asked his doctor if it was possible to develop pulmonary emboli from great stress. His doctor, a cardiologist, said, "Yes. Definitely."

We discussed how the body reacts to stress — my own hypothesis is that changes in body chemistry when under stress can cause the blood to thicken, and clots can form — causing heart attacks, strokes, and pulmonary emboli. And yes — these can be fatal!

She now has a new cat that she loves. And now she understands that she needs to learn some new coping strategies to reduce her stress levels before she endangers her health and her life.

(Note: I discussed this situation with another physician who specializes in pulmonary diseases. He stated that due to both siblings getting pulmonary emboli so young, that it is genetic in causation.

Another doctor — an internal medicine physician who has a family practice — claims genetics plays a small part in many diseases compared to the life style choices one makes over years — things like diet, exercise, attitude, supplements, smoking, alcohol use, etc. Genetics we can't control — but life style choices are under our choices and decisions.)

———————————

God, grant me the serenity to accept the things I cannot change, the courage to change the things I can, and the wisdom to know the difference.

— The Serenity Prayer

22. Chronic Illness
From my sister, Beula Peele

Tick, tick, tick — my biological clock was keeping time with the milestones in my life. I was in a stable, satisfying 30-year marriage. We had given our son and daughter both roots and wings. They were happily married and pursuing dreams of their own. I was employed as a medical social worker in a small rural hospital. My job at Page Memorial was both rewarding and quite challenging. We were nestled in the heart of the lovely Shenandoah Valley, surrounded by majestic mountains, kind neighbors and friends. We were in God's country, living among God's people. The one dark cloud that billowed over our heads was a significant mortgage on our home.

Both of us enjoyed relatively good health, however, only the normal aging concerns of sixty year olds. Things looked fine, except for this slight tremor that was gradually increasing on my left side. Dr. Perdue, a neurologist, was monitoring it once a year. We had discussed the various possible diagnoses. Then came the day he "called it." I listened quietly as he gently informed me, "You have Parkinson's." He followed this with his plans for treatment. He ended the visit by taking a book off his shelf and handing it to me to read until my next visit several weeks later. Even though I had known Parkinson's was a possibility, the reality of it now hit me like an icy wind gust on a January day. One is never quite prepared for such a shock.

Parkinson's, a chronic, long-term progressive disease that slowly but surely will debilitate me, is now in my system. I work in the health care scene every day. Daily as a social worker I provide support and assistance to people with diseases and handicaps. Suddenly I find myself on the receiving end. It is time to apply my social work skills to myself. The next few weeks are a blur with diverse responses within me. A garden variety of questions, thoughts, and feelings dash madly through me. This can't be me! Maybe the doc is wrong in his diagnosis — sometimes they are. I stumble blindly from denial to the "why me?" search. From here I give myself permission to grieve my future, but certain, loss. Slowly, but inevitably my life will change as my functioning skills deteriorate. My dream of aging gracefully is not in the cards for me. My cherished love of independence will crumble around me, as helplessness displaces my independent spirit. Tears of sadness mingle with tears of anger at this great injustice. All the why questions keep popping up. And God — where on earth is He when I need Him?

While trying to process my reactions, I began sharing with my spouse, Fred; children, Autumn and Sterling, and with their spouses, Paul and Meridith; sister, Rhoda; friends, neighbors and coworkers. All were supportive, offering comfort and encouragement. My family physician, Dr. Morgan, was informed and began working with Dr. Perdue.

The weeks rolled by and it was time to return to Dr. Perdue. He had prescribed medication to control the symptoms. There is no cure. He had started with a low dosage to see how I tolerated it. This would be increased as required, and as my tolerance permitted. We talked some more, our dialogue consisting of questions and answers. He increased the dosage and we discussed side effects. I felt encouraged as he told me potential results and time frames. We talked about productive years ahead with appropriate treatment. I began to feel some attitudes of gratitude; at least I did not have MS. Neither was I in pain. With his help I could enjoy some quality of life yet. I resolved to learn as much about my disease as I could and try to take it one day at a time. I found a Parkinson's support group. Fred and I joined other patients and their spouses. This provided information, support and socialization.

Alone with myself, I took time to reflect. At sixty-two years I had a vast storehouse of memories I could take out and savor. As a social worker, how would I help a client face this future? Now was the time to use these skills on myself. My adult life has been filled with many happy events, the love of family and friends, meaning and purpose in my life. God had been good to me, filling my life with blessings and joys. Even now, with the help of Dr. Perdue and the medications, I would still have some time to enjoy life. I needed to focus on what was left rather than what was gone. It was up to me. I still had some control over this horrible disease, even if all I could control was my attitude toward it. I would surround myself with positive people, atmospheres, and experiences. I would work to keep my spirits up. I also vowed to be gentle with myself. When the discouraging times come, as they undoubtedly will, I will allow myself to grieve, and avoid critical feedback.

★　★　★　★　★　★　★

Having made this commitment to myself, I proceeded to take special notice of beauty and joy around me. I have a cat, Junette, that I dearly love. She reciprocates with love for me in her own unique way. I began taking special pleasure in her. I enjoy classical music and quality singing. I take extra delight in listening to it now. I go over a mountain to work — it's a forty-five minute drive. I have never minded the drive, but now I've begun to savor each stretch of its beauty. I enjoy the strength, peace, grandeur and stability of the mountains. I take great pleasure in a weekend drive among the West Virginia mountains or going up on the Skyline Drive of Virginia. Fred drives and together we listen to music, converse or just quietly enjoy the outdoor beauty. In my work at the hospital, I try extra hard to focus on patients' needs and provide for them with exceptional services. I try to give them the quality of care I may some day need myself. In my home, I have some recently inherited antiques from my parents. I especially enjoy the dishes. Fred and I take time to entertain on occasions. I dress up the table with pretty decorations, and serve good food on my grandmother's antique china. Then we linger at the table with guests, just enjoying the conversation and their friendship. I get letters in the mail from friends and family. I read them with delight, knowing they care for me. Rhoda and a friend, Jean, from college days, are particularly regular in their correspondence.

Sometime in the future I will not be able to do these things. Some day I will also need to resign from Page Memorial Hospital. But I will have stored away many memories of these happy times. I know the statistics are that 40% of people with Parkinson's develop dementia. This upsets me if I dwell on it. I try not to; or else I maintain hope that I'll be in the 60%. I know I can trust Fred to make good decisions about me and for me as I deteriorate. I work hard every day at remaining positive and finding joy. I use humor and find reasons to chuckle, even at myself.

Sometimes I have setbacks that I can't control. One of these was when Dr. Perdue added a new medication, as he had determined that I was "under medicated." I began the medication on the weekend due to concern with side effects and not wanting to miss work. I did get sick on it. Fred was attentive and Junette kept walking all around my head purring and touching my face with her nose as I lay on the bed. She also lay down beside me as close as she could get. When I was feeling better the next day, she returned to her usual behaviors. My body did adjust to the new medication, and it reduced my symptoms. I know there will continue to be setbacks as the disease progresses. I will allow myself to grieve the loss. But I will also try to focus on what remains, while I remember the good times.

My life has already changed, and it will keep changing. I will deteriorate. That is a reality for me. But I will work on my attitude and try to be proactive. I have a cane that I keep in the car for any outdoor walking, as I am losing my sense of balance. I now use a shower bench as I am in danger of falling when bathing. I have more problems with memory and so I write down more details at work. Due to some deterioration of my fine motor skills, I sometimes need help with such things as blouse buttons and earrings. Fred helps me at these times. But I am still working full time, driving, entertaining, and enjoying life, family and friends. Little things like the fire blazing in the fireplace while reading or watching a TV show with Fred are still pleasurable. An email from my daughter, sister, or a friend, being invited to my son's home for dinner and a movie with him and his wife, all bring joy to me. I allow myself more time to get dressed — but I do get dressed and go out. When I'm driving I need to park in a fashion that I can get out of my car. But there are handicapped spots to use and I can still go out independently. My life has indeed changed. But God is still there for me, and He will carry me through this experience. My walk is a walk of faith in the dark. I am redefining what is important to me, and I will need to keep redefining this as I deteriorate.

Now I explore and draw on my available sources of comfort and strength. Certainly God is one of these, even though my why questions have not yet been answered. One day He'll call me "home" and it won't matter. For now, I'll have to trust him. I know Fred can be counted on as I deteriorate. We will soon be checking with an attorney whose area of expertise is geriatric law, and making some decisions.

But, I have time yet. The mountains continue to be a source of comfort and strength to me. My children and their spouses are supportive and will do what they can — if only able to provide emotional support. Junette will continue to bring me pleasure. Her antics will both entertain and amuse me. Neighbors and friends will still care about me. One of my friends is a therapist. When I need it, she will continue to put on her "therapist hat" and provide that service to me. Rhoda will continue to nurture and encourage me. Fred and I attend a small country church nestled among the hills around our home. I have friends from another church in the same locality. These people all care about me. I have pastoral support I can count on to nurture me spiritually. People at my hospital offer their support, expertise and friendship. I have a good working relationship with my physicians. Then at the close of the day, I can curl up on the sofa with a bowl of fresh fruit and watch a movie with Fred. When I have a bad day, I can grieve and know that tomorrow is another day and may be better. I'll be OK.

Strength does not come from winning. Your struggles develop your strengths. When you go through hardships and decide not to surrender, that is strength.

— Arnold Schwarzenegger

The Sandbox
From *Daily Insights* sent by Bob Proctor

A little boy was spending his Saturday morning playing in his sandbox. He had with him his box of cars and trucks, his plastic pail, and a shiny, red plastic shovel. In the process of creating roads and tunnels in the soft sand, he discovered a large rock in the middle of the sandbox.

The lad dug around the rock, managing to dislodge it from the dirt. With no little bit of struggle, he pushed and nudged the rock across the sandbox by using his feet. (He was a very small boy and the rock was very large.) When the boy got the rock to the edge of the sandbox, however, he found that he couldn't roll it up and over the wall.

Determined, the little boy shoved, pushed, and pried, but every time he thought he had made some progress, the rock tipped and then fell back into the sandbox. The little boy grunted, struggled, pushed, and shoved. But his only reward was to have the rock roll back, smashing his fingers. Finally he burst into tears of frustration.

All this time the boy's father watched from his living room window as the drama unfolded. At the moment the tears fell, a large shadow fell across the boy and the sandbox. It was the boy's father. Gently but firmly he said, "Son, why didn't you use all the strength that you had available?" Defeated the boy sobbed back, "But I did, Daddy, I did! I used all the strength that I had!"

"No son," corrected the father kindly, "You didn't use all the strength you had. You didn't ask me for help." With that the father reached down, picked up the rock, and removed it from the sandbox. It is amazing what we can accomplish if we just ask for a little help.

Go to www.rhodasearcy.com for FREE Daily Insights.

23. The Birdies

From an email; author unknown

On July 22 I was enroute to Washington, D.C., for a business trip. It was all so very ordinary, until we landed in Denver for a plane change. As I collected my belongings from the overhead bin, an announcement was made for Mr. Lloyd Glenn to see the United Customer Service Representative immediately. I thought nothing of it until I reached the door to leave the plane, and I heard a gentleman asking every male if he was Mr. Glenn. At this point I knew something was wrong, and my heart sank.

When I got off the plane a solemn-faced young man came toward me and said, "Mr. Glenn, there is an emergency at your home. I do not know what the emergency is, or who is involved, but I will take you to the phone so you can call the hospital." My heart was now pounding, but the will to be calm took over.

Woodenly, I followed this stranger to the distant telephone, where I called the number he gave me for the Mission Hospital. My call was put through to the trauma center, where I learned that my three-year-old son had been trapped underneath the automatic garage door for several minutes, and that when my wife had found him he was dead. CPR had been performed by a neighbor, who is a doctor, and the paramedics had continued the treatment as Brian was transported to the hospital.

By the time of my call, Brian was revived and they believed he would live, but they did not know how much damage had been done to his brain, nor to his heart. They explained that the door had completely closed on his little sternum right over his heart. He had been severely crushed. After speaking with the medical staff, my wife sounded worried but not hysterical, and I took comfort in her calmness. The return flight seemed to last forever, but finally I arrived at the hospital six hours after the garage door had come down.

When I walked into the intensive care unit, nothing could have prepared me to see my little son lying so still on a great big bed with tubes and monitors everywhere. He was on a respirator. I glanced at my wife, who stood and tried to give me a reassuring smile.

It all seemed like a terrible dream. I was filled in with the details and given a guarded prognosis. Brian was going to live, and the preliminary tests indicated that his heart was OK, two miracles in one and of themselves. But only time would tell if his brain received any damage.

Throughout the seemingly endless hours, my wife was calm. She felt that Brian would eventually be all right. I hung on to her words and faith like a lifeline. All that night and the next day Brian remained unconscious. It seemed like forever since I had left for my business trip the day before.

Finally at two o'clock that afternoon, our son regained consciousness and sat up uttering the most beautiful words I have ever heard spoken. He said, "Daddy, hold me" and reached for me with his little arms.

By the next day he was pronounced as having no neurological or physical deficits, and the story of his miraculous survival spread throughout the hospital. You cannot imagine how we felt as we took Brian home. We felt a unique reverence for life and the love of our Heavenly Father that comes to those who brush death so closely.

In the days that followed there was a special spirit about our home. Our two older children were much closer to their little brother. My wife and I were much closer to each other, and all of us were very close as a whole family. Life took on a less stressful pace. Perspective seemed to be more focused, and balance much easier to gain and maintain. We felt deeply blessed. Our gratitude was truly profound.

The story is not over (smile)! Almost a month later to the day of the accident, Brian awoke from his afternoon nap and said, "Sit down, Mommy. I have something to tell you." At this time in his life, Brian usually spoke in small phrases; so to say a large sentence surprised my wife. She sat down with him on his bed, and he began his sacred and remarkable story.

"Do you remember when I got stuck under the garage door? Well, it was so heavy and it hurt really bad. I called to you, but you couldn't hear me. I started to cry, but then it hurt too bad. And then the 'birdies' came."

"The birdies?" my wife asked, puzzled.

"Yes," he replied. "The birdies made a whooshing sound and flew into the garage. They took care of me."

"They did?"

"Yes," he said. "One of the birdies came and got you. She came to tell you I got stuck under the door."

A sweet reverent feeling filled the room. The spirit was so strong and yet lighter than air. My wife realized that a three-year-old had no concept of death and spirits, so he was referring to the beings who came to him from beyond as "birdies" because they were up in the air like birds that fly.

"What did the birdies look like?" she asked.

Brian answered, "They were so beautiful. They were dressed in white, all white. Some of them had green and white. But some of them had on just white."

"Did they say anything?"

"Yes," he answered. "They told me the baby would be all right."

"The baby?" my wife asked, confused.

Brian answered. "The baby lying on the garage floor." He went on, "You came out and opened the garage door and ran to the baby. You told the baby to stay and not leave."

My wife nearly collapsed upon hearing this, for she had indeed gone and knelt beside Brian's body and, seeing his crushed chest, whispered, "Don't leave us Brian, please stay if you can."

As she listened to Brian telling her the words she had spoken, she realized that the spirit had left his body and was looking down from above on this little lifeless form.

"Then what happened?" she asked.

"We went on a trip," he said. "Far, far away." He grew agitated trying to say the things he didn't seem to have the words for. My wife tried to calm and comfort him and let him know it would be okay. He struggled with wanting to tell something that obviously was very important to him, but finding the words was difficult. "We flew so fast up in the air. They're so pretty, Mommy." And he added, "And there are lots and lots of birdies."

My wife was stunned. Into her mind the sweet comforting spirit enveloped her more soundly, but with an urgency she had never before known. Brian went on to tell her that the "birdies" had told him that he had to come back and tell everyone about the "birdies."

He said they brought him back to the house and that a big fire truck and an ambulance were there. A man was bringing the baby out on a white bed and he tried to tell the man that the baby would be okay, but the man couldn't hear him. He said the birdies told him he had to go with the ambulance, but they would be near him. He said they were so pretty and so peaceful, and he didn't want to come back.

Then the bright light came. He said that the light was so bright and so warm, and he loved the bright light so much. Someone was in the bright light and put their arms around him and told him, "I love you but you have to go back. You have to play baseball and tell everyone about the birdies." Then the person in the bright light kissed him and waved bye-bye. Then whoosh, the big sound came and they went into the clouds.

The story went on for an hour. He taught us that "bird-ies" were always with us, but we don't see them because we look with our eyes and we don't hear them because we listen with our ears. But they are always there. You can only see them in here (he put his hand over his heart). They whisper the things to help us to do what is right because they love us so much. Brian continued, stating, "I have a plan, Mommy. You have a plan. Daddy has a plan. Everyone has a plan. We must all live our plan and keep our promises. The birdies help us to do that 'cause they love us so much."

In the weeks that followed, he often came to us and told all, or part of it, again and again. Always the story remained the same. The details were never changed or out of order. A few times he added further bits of information and clarified the message he had already delivered. It never ceased to amaze us how he could tell such detail and speak beyond his ability when he talked about his birdies.

Everywhere he went, he told strangers about the "bird-ies." Surprisingly, no one ever looked at him strangely when he did this. Rather, they always got a softened look on their face and smiled.

Needless to say, we have not been the same ever since that day, and I pray we never will be.

———

Do not save your loving speeches for your friends til they are dead; do not write them on their tombstones, speak them rather now instead.

— Anna Cummins

When Sudden Terror Tears Apart

Carl P. Daw, Jr.

When sudden terror tears apart
the world we thought was ours,
we find how fragile strength can be,
how limited our powers.

As tower and fortress fall, we watch
with disbelieving stare
and numbly hear the anguished cries
that pierce the ash-filled air.

Yet most of all we are aware
of emptiness and void;
of lives cut short, of structures razed,
of confidence destroyed.

From this abyss of doubt and fear
we grope for words to pray,
and hear our stammering tongues embrace
a timeless Kyrie.

Have mercy, Lord, give strength and peace,
and make our courage great;
restrain our urge to seek revenge,
to turn our heart to hate.

Help us to know your steadfast love,
your presence near as breath;
rekindle in our hearts the hope
of life that conquers death.

24. Missouri Sends Response Team to Ground Zero

From Dr. Nancy O'Reilly

On September 10, 2001, Dr. Nancy O'Reilly, Psy.D., was a member of the Crisis Team of the Ozarks that enrolled in an intensive five-day training given by the National Organization of Victim Assistance (NOVA). Besides Dr. O'Reilly, participants hailed from law enforcement, fire and rescue, social services, disaster relief and emergency management. The Crisis Team wanted to hone its effectiveness for crisis intervention following a disaster. Other NOVA teams had helped survivors cope with horror following the Oklahoma City bombings, the Columbine, Colorado shootings, and the war in Bosnia.

On September 11, 2001, while getting ready to return for the second day of NOVA training, in shock and disbelief, Dr. O'Reilly watched the televised explosions of the World Trade Center and Pentagon. The entire team decided to continue with the training, realizing how timely their skills would be in assisting the recovery of Americans.

On October 12, 2001, Dr. O'Reilly and seven other members of the Crisis Team of the Ozarks were asked by NOVA to respond to the aftermath of the terrorist attack. NOVA teams from New Jersey, New York, Texas, Ohio, Tennessee, Iowa, and Florida as well as Missouri launched a joint effort.

From the New Jersey Family Assistance Center, Dr. O'Reilly's team accompanied families of those missing or deceased on a pilgrimage by ferry across the Hudson River to the World Trade Center site. On the ferry, they put on hard hats, goggles, and masks. They were given red, white, and blue carnations and teddy bears. They shared their family's story and grief while the American Red Cross served a meal.

Once in New York, escorted by police, the families spent about fifteen minutes on a platform overlooking the site. Many National Guard and recovery workers stopped, removed their hats, saluted, and placed their hands over their hearts. Many called it, "Ground Hero."

Seeing the devastation, many victims felt this was the closest they would ever be to their missing loved one. They realized that this was "goodbye"; he or she would not be coming home. As it was a crime scene, pictures or remembrances were not permitted. But nearby a memorial had been constructed by those leaving flowers, hand written messages, poems, prayers, children's drawings, teddy bears, pictures and memorabilia.

The families returned to the New Jersey Family Assistance Center, which was established by the governor immediately after the attacks; there fifteen victims' aid services were available. The Missouri Crisis Team stayed with the families during their eight-hour ordeal. They helped victims' families file for death certificates or begin the process of applying for assistance from FEMA, the Red Cross, or the Salvation Army.

For sixteen days, Dr. O'Reilly experienced an array of emotions. "Words cannot express what I have seen and the pain I have shared, but there have been many joys as well — hugs, thank-you's, smiles on children's faces, knowing that we have helped those who needed resources. I am changed forever," she reported. "I cannot believe I was there yet I cannot believe I left. What I have learned is to pray for each other, hold those you love close to you, and live each day with great vigor and joy."

Used with Permission from Dr. Nancy O'Reilly's website: www.womenspeak.com.

One
From an email after 9-11-01

As the soot and dirt and ash rained down,
We became one color.

As we carried each other down the stairs of the burning building,
We became one class.

As we lit candles of waiting and hope,
We became one generation.

As the firefighters and police officers fought their way into the inferno,
We became one gender.

As we fell to our knees in prayer for strength,
We became one faith.

As we whispered or shouted words of encouragement,
We spoke one language.

As we gave our blood in lines a mile long,
We became one body.

As we mourned together the great loss,
We became one family.

As we cried tears of grief and loss,
We became one soul.

As we retell with pride of the sacrifice of heroes,
We become one people.

We are:
One color
One class
One generation
One gender
One faith
One language
One body
One family
One soul
One people

We are The Power of One.
We are United.
We are America.

— Author unknown

25. "I'm Staying Navy!"
From an email

During the last few weeks, I think all of us have heard some extraordinary stories about how wonderful our country is. I was particularly moved by the following letter from one of our service personnel and how another nation, that was once our enemy, is supporting our efforts. Here is the letter. This is an e-mail from a young ensign aboard the *USS Winston Churchill* (DDG-81) to his parents. (*Churchill* is an Arleigh Burke class AEGIS guided missile destroyer, commissioned March 10, 2001, and is the only active US navy warship named after a foreign national.)

October 10, 2001
Dear Dad,

We are at sea. The remainder of our port visits have all been cancelled. We have spent every day since the attacks going back and forth within imaginary boxes drawn in the ocean, standing high-security watches, and trying to make the best of it. We have seen the articles and photographs, and they are sickening. Being isolated, I don't think we appreciate the full scope of what is happening back home, but we are definitely feeling the effects. About two hours ago, we were hailed by a German Navy destroyer, the *Lutjens*, requesting permission to pass close by our port side. Strange, since we're in the middle of an empty ocean, but the captain acquiesced and we prepared to render them honors from our bridge wing. As they were making their approach, our conning officer used binoculars and announced that the *Lutjens* was flying, not the German, but the American flag. As she came alongside us, we saw the American flag flying at half-mast and her entire crew topside standing at silent, rigid attention in their dress uniforms. They had made a sign that was displayed on her side that read, "We Stand By You." There was not a dry eye on the bridge as they stayed alongside of us for a few minutes and saluted. It was the most powerful thing I have seen in my life. The German Navy did an incredible thing for this crew, and it has truly been the highest point in the days since the attacks. It's amazing to think that only a half-century ago things were quite different. After the *Lutjens* pulled away, the officer of the deck, who had been planning to get out later this year, turned to me and said, "I'm staying Navy!" I'll write you when I know more about when I'll be home, but this is it for now.

Love you guys.——-

Gary Olene

———————

Your work is to discover your work and then with all your heart give yourself to it.

— Buddha

26. Making a Difference
From an email; author unknown

Who you are and what you do makes a difference! One of the human psychological hungers is for recognition and acknowledgement. Dr. Eric Berne called this "stroke hunger."

A high school teacher in New York decided to honor each of her seniors by telling them the difference each of them made. She called her students to the front of the class, one at a time. First, she told each one how he or she had made a difference to her and the class. Then she presented each of them with a blue ribbon imprinted with gold letters which read, "Who I Am Makes a Difference."

Afterwards, the teacher decided to do a class project to see what kind of impact recognition would have on a community. She gave the students three more ribbons each and instructed them to go out and spread this acknowledgement ceremony. Then they were to follow up on the results, see who honored whom, and report back to the class in about a week.

One of the boys in the class went to a junior executive in a nearby company and honored him for helping him with his career planning. He gave him a blue ribbon and put it on his shirt. Then he gave him two extra ribbons and said, "We're doing a class project on recognition. We'd like you to go out, find someone to honor, give them a blue ribbon, then give them the extra ribbon so they can acknowledge a third person to keep this acknowledgement ceremony going. Then please report back to me and tell me what happened."

Later that day the junior executive went in to see his boss, who had been noted, by the way, as being kind of a grouchy fellow. He sat his boss down. He told him that he deeply admired him for being a creative genius. The boss seemed very surprised. The junior executive asked if he would accept the gift of the blue ribbon and would he give him permission to put it on him. His surprised boss said, "Well, sure." The junior executive took the blue ribbon and placed it right on his boss's jacket above his heart. Then as he gave him the extra ribbon, he said, "Would you do me a favor? Would you take this extra ribbon and pass it on by honoring someone else? The young boy who first gave me these ribbons is doing a project in school and we want to keep this recognition ceremony going and find out how it affects people."

That night the boss came home to his fourteen-year-old son and sat him down. He said, "The most incredible thing happened to me today. I was in my office and one of the junior executives came in and told me he admired me and gave me a blue ribbon for being a creative genius. Imagine! He thinks I'm a creative genius! Then he put this blue ribbon that says, 'Who I Am Makes a Difference' on my jacket above my heart. He gave me an extra ribbon and asked me to find somebody else to honor. As I was driving home tonight, I started thinking about whom I would honor with this ribbon. I thought about you. I want to honor you. My days are really hectic, and when I come home I don't pay a lot of attention to you. Sometimes I scream at you for not getting good enough grades in school and for your bedroom being a mess, but somehow, tonight I just wanted to sit here and, well, just let you know you are the most important person in my life. You're a great kid, and I love you!"

The startled boy started to sob and sob, and he couldn't stop crying. His whole body shook. He looked up at his father and said through his tears, "Dad, earlier tonight I sat in my room and wrote a letter to you and Mom explaining why I had killed myself and asking you to forgive me. I was going to commit suicide tonight after you were asleep. I just didn't think that you cared at all. The letter is upstairs. Now I don't need it." His father walked upstairs and found a heartfelt letter full of anguish and pain. The envelope was addressed "Mom and Dad."

The boss went back to work a changed man. He was no longer a grouch, but made sure he let all his employees know that they made a difference. The junior executive helped several other young people with career planning and never forgot to let them know that they made a difference in his life...one being the boss's son. And the young boy and his classmates learned a valuable lesson. Who you are—and passing it on—does make a difference.

27. A Red Marble

From an email as well as *Daily Insights* by Bob Proctor

During the waning years of the Depression in a small southeastern Idaho community, I used to stop by Mr. Miller's roadside stand for farm fresh produce as the season made it available. Food and money were still extremely scarce and bartering was used, extensively.

One day Mr. Miller was bagging some early potatoes for me. I noticed a small boy, delicate of bone and feature, ragged but clean, hungrily apprising a basket of freshly picked green peas. I paid for my potatoes but was also drawn to the display of fresh green peas.

I am a pushover for creamed peas and new potatoes. Pondering the peas, I couldn't help overhearing the conversation between Mr. Miller and the ragged boy next to me.

"Hello Barry, how are you today?"

"Hello Mr. Miller. Fine, thank you. Just admiring those peas...sure look good."

"They are good, Barry. How's your Mother?"

"Fine. Getting stronger all the time."

"Good. Anything I can help you with?"

"No, Sir. Just admiring those peas."

"Would you like to take some home?"

"No, Sir. I don't have anything to pay for them with."

"Well, what have you to trade me for some of those peas?"

"All I have is my prize marble here."

"Is that right? Let me see it."

"Here it is. She's a dandy."

"I can see that. Hmmmm, only thing is, this one is blue and I sort of go for red. Do you have a red one like this at home?"

"Not exactly...but almost."

"Tell you what. Take this sack of peas home with you and next trip this way let me look at that red marble."

"Sure will. Thanks, Mr. Miller."

Mrs. Miller, who had been standing nearby, came over to help me. With a smile she said: "There are two other boys like him in our community; all three are in very poor circumstances. Jim just loves to bargain with them for peas, apples, tomatoes, or whatever."

"When they come back with their red marbles, and they always do, he decides he doesn't like red after all and he sends them home with a bag of produce for a green marble or an orange one, perhaps."

I left the stand, smiling to myself, impressed. A short time later I moved to Utah, but I never forgot the story of Mr. Miller, the boys and their bartering.

Several years went by, each more rapidly than the previous one. Just recently I had occasion to visit some old friends in that Idaho community, and while I was there I learned that Mr. Miller had died. They were having his viewing that evening, and knowing my friends wanted to go, I agreed to accompany them. Upon arrival at the mortuary we fell into line to meet the relatives of the deceased and to offer whatever comfort we could.

Ahead of us in line were three young men. One was in an army uniform and the other two wore nice haircuts, dark suits, and white shirts...very professional looking. They approached Mrs. Miller, standing smiling and composed by her husband's casket. Each of the young men hugged her, kissed her on the cheek, spoke briefly with her and moved on to the casket. Her misty light blue eyes followed them as, one by one, each young man stopped briefly and placed his own warm hand over the cold pale hand in the casket. Each left the mortuary, awkwardly, wiping his eyes. Our turn came to meet Mrs. Miller.

I told her who I was and mentioned the story she had

told me about the marbles. Eyes glistening, she took my hand and led me to the casket. "Those three young men that just left were the boys I told you about. They just told me how they appreciated the things Jim "traded" them. Now, at last, when Jim could not change his mind about color or size...they came to pay their debt.

"We've never had a great deal of wealth in this world," she confided, "but right now Jim would consider himself the richest man in Idaho."

With loving gentleness she lifted the lifeless fingers of her deceased husband. Resting underneath were three magnificently shiny red marbles.

— Author unknown

Go to www.rhodasearcy.com to register for FREE Daily Insights.

———————————

Believe it can be done. When you believe something can be done, really believe, your mind will find the ways to do it. Believing a solution paves the way to solution.

— Dr. David Schwartz, Author of *The Magic of Thinking Big*

PART TWO

STRATEGIES

It is not because things are difficult
that we do not dare; it is because
we do not dare that things are difficult.

— Seneca, Roman Philosopher

Understanding Change and Crisis

Change is both certain and inevitable, though often sudden and unpredictable. Most people welcome positive changes, such as graduations, weddings, births, or even the coming of Spring after a bleak winter. Some people love change and create it for pleasure, excitement, and growth. These are risk takers. For others, change can be more difficult to adjust to and may even be avoided or resisted, especially if they have not had time to prepare themselves. Changes that are predictable are often easier to deal with than those that are unexpected. Even the risk takers resist changes that are sprung on them without their input. How change enters our lives and our personal makeup are key factors in how we cope and how we respond initially and long term.

Change can be both evolutionary or gradual in nature, and revolutionary or sudden in nature. Evolutionary change occurs over a period of time, and is more gradual and less shocking or disruptive. It goes on often without our awareness or conscious thought, until something happens that brings it to our attention. An example would be the gradual extinction of a species, or the social and familial changes that can occur over decades or generations.

On the other hand, revolutionary change—sudden, shocking, dramatic, and disruptive—requires massive response from individuals and society as a whole. Many individuals have initiated change on this magnitude, sometimes knowingly and other times in hindsight. When revolutionary change occurs, everyone's paradigms shift. The terrorist attacks on September 11, 2001 created such a shift: safety and security issues have emerged juxtaposed with an expectation for freedom in America.

Other changes are developmental/maturational and situational. Maturational changes are expected, have an internal cause, and relate to the life cycle. They include events like starting school, puberty, graduation, marriage, choice of career, menopause, retirement, and aging. Families go through phases from marriage to death of a spouse. When something occurs at any of these stages that is "outside" the norm or expected process, people often experience it as a loss or change, which is a negative factor. Examples include a child dying before a parent, a marriage ending in divorce, or a breadwinner losing a job. All of these—though part of life—are not the usual progression we expect to occur in our lives. We may also experience moving from one stage to another as difficult when we are not adequately prepared for the change.

Situational changes are not specifically related to the stages of the life cycle, though they may accompany life cycle changes. They involve a sudden loss or threatened loss, such as status loss or change (e.g. job or position), loss of a loved one, loss of physical abilities, etc. Situational changes are accidental, unexpected, and have an external cause.

People in all cultures experience change through the life cycles, evolution and revolution, and specific situations. Significant Emotional Events, or "SEE"s, create the greatest changes of all. They create crises in our lives, changing how we perceive ourselves and our world, and requiring a revised identity for one's self and one's place in the world. Often these SEE events combine both internal and

---

If fear is cultivated it will become stronger. If faith is cultivated it will achieve mastery.

— John Paul Jones

external factors that interact to intensify the process of change.

A crisis is defined as 1) disequilibrium, with usual coping patterns short-circuited; 2) a turning point in life, for the better or the worse, and 3) an obstacle to important life goals, that is, for a time, insurmountable through use of the usual problem-solving mechanisms. A period of disorganization ensues, during which many different abortive attempts at solutions are made. Eventually, some kind of adaptation is achieved that may or may not be in the best interest of that person and his surrounding relationships. Crises are self-limiting; they cause a temporary loss of the ability to cope; a lack of ability to use usual support systems (both internal and external), and a reduction of energy (due to withdrawal from or denial of the problem) or redirection of energy to random or seemingly non-goal-directed behaviors.

Typically, people have one of several attitudinal responses to change. They may *deny* the change exists, such as Roger initially did in an earlier story, or just not see it, as my father did when my mother was dying with metastatic bone cancer. They may *avoid* the reality or meaning of the change. Many people who have early symptoms of cancer may hold this attitude, avoiding contact with a doctor until the disease has progressed. A worker may observe others being laid off but avoid facing the reality that the company has financial problems.

Some people *react* to the change. Often the bearer of the bad message receives the brunt of the reaction, which may be anger or hostility or other grief responses. For instance, families may respond with anger to a doctor who informs them of their loved one's terminal illness. Since reacting with emotional responses is essential to process grief, this is often a healthier response in the long term, though difficult for the bearer of the message to absorb and handle.

Some people *accept* the change. They may have seen it coming, or they may accept it after a period of grief and dealing with their feelings. Some people temporarily accept the change initially, because they have to focus on other more pressing issues at the time. However, these individuals may later find themselves experiencing Post Traumatic Stress Disorder (see page 196)—a delayed response to the situation that may show up months or even years later.

Over time, people *incorporate* the new situation and reality. For example, at a recent graduation event, my sister, who has Parkinson's Disease, borrowed a wheelchair so she did not have to walk the half-mile or more to the stadium in the crowd of thousands. She can walk that distance and wants to maintain her independence, but under certain circumstances she *adjusts* to handle her slower, more deliberate walking. *Adjustments* to change can be done in either life-promoting or life-destroying ways. Refusing to go to crowded events would be life-destroying for her, because she would no longer be a participant in significant family events that matter deeply to her. People who accept and incorporate change often eventually find—to their surprise — that "Wow! This changed my life for the better!"

Not all changes are perceived as a crisis. The Chinese symbol for crisis means "opportunity." The symbol contains two characters: one represents danger; the second, opportunity. So we see that a crisis can have two sides: the change can become an opportunity or challenge for the person experiencing it, or it can become a threat, generating fear, anxiety, and potential danger. Crises experiences are a *normal* part of life, and we experience the change on many levels. It is like a pebble thrown into a still lake, with the ripples extending outward in ever-enlarging circles. If the pebble is instead a boulder, then the concentric circles are deeper and wider and faster! Or if there are many pebbles or boulders at one time, the ripples become huge waves that threaten our very existence. So it is when change—crisis—intrudes into our lives. Crises experiences become both a separation (letting go) and a refocusing.

Perhaps the most exciting and hopeful aspect of a crisis is that these experiences provide an opportunity for growth. Previous unresolved issues often resurface during a crisis and provide an opportunity to develop new problem-solving skills and abilities. This not only assists us to resolve change and loss in the present situation, but also provides an opportunity to return to and "clean out" unfinished business that has clogged our emotions and limited our functioning as a fully-human being.

A crisis has three distinct phases: the initial (shock), the middle (suffering), and the ending (resolution). The emotional intensity of the crisis is usually resolved in four to six weeks, and occasionally may be shorter for some people. Major losses or crises, however, such as the death of a child or spouse, take longer for resolution. When someone has multiple major losses or crises in different aspects of his life, the process of recovery may extend over years, or a person may emotionally "bury" the situation and on the surface appear to be in resolution until another change event occurs and brings the earlier crises to the surface. We have seen this process occur in veterans of war, or rape or violence victims, or holocaust survivors. The phases of a crisis are not clearly demarcated, but rather seesaw back and forth and provide an emotional roller coaster type of ride with varying levels of emotional intensity.

All crisis situations contain elements of normal

Even in your old age, I am He, And even to gray hairs I will carry you! I have made, and I will bear, Even I will carry, and will deliver you.

— Isaiah 46:4

grieving over losses. When people grieve over a real or perceived loss (and to the person, perceived loss is experienced as actual loss), they go through various steps to reach resolution. The grieving person realizes his dependency on the person or situation or object of grief, and his state of well-being and effective functioning is disrupted. Initially, the person attempts to refute, deny or dispute the reality of the loss. She feels impotent, lost, and helpless, and how she sends out behavioral cries for help—and the responses, or lack of responses, from others—has significant implications for recovery. A failure or inability to emit the cry or to elicit an appropriate response will create a delay in recovery. The person attempts to mentally reconstitute a representation of the lost person (or situation or item). A painful process of separating and dissecting the bitter and the sweet memories ensues, before the mourner ultimately comes to peace with herself and the new state of life.

We might compare the grieving process to the healing process of a physical wound. The whole body has to respond appropriately to activate the healing response. Initially, life itself may be threatened. After the initial shock on the body's systems, if the systems can be stabilized and the right healing ingredients are available to the body (water, nutrition, electrolytes), the body's natural healing forces take over. However, medical interventions will still be needed.

Assessing mental, emotional, and social progress of the grieving process is more difficult than assessing the healing progress of a physical wound, but it is just as essential. It requires care, attention, and patience. The healing process—whether of a physical wound or a grieving person—cannot be hurried or accelerated by outside forces. What is essential is providing needed resources for the person or body to create its own healing process.

George L. Engel wrote an article, "Grief and Grieving" in the *American Journal of Nursing* in 1964, which outlines the five stages in healing grief. Initially, there is *disbelief*, a denial or refusal of the fact, followed by numbness and a stunned reaction. Most Americans can identify with this stage as they recall their first exposure to the images of terrorist attacks on September 11, 2001. This is followed with brief flashes of despair and anguish as reality penetrates. Normal behavior at this disbelief stage is to attempt to protect oneself against the effects of the overwhelming stress by raising the threshold against its recognition or against the painful feelings evoked. Sometimes there is an overt intellectual acceptance of reality; however, the emotional aspects are denied. Those who served at Ground Zero in New York or the Pentagon functioned with this intellectual acceptance in order to act effectively in saving lives as the buildings collapsed or in aiding later recovery.

The second stage is *developing awareness*, which begins minutes to hours after the initial stage. Reality penetrates into consciousness, and the victim expresses an acute and increasing awareness of the anguish of the loss, or an empty feeling. He may experience anger toward self and others. Crying serves to acknowledge and communicate the loss by regressing to a more helpless and childlike state. The suppression of tears or inability to cry may occur when the loss is associated with ambivalence or the survivor experiences much guilt and shame.

The third stage, *restitution*, is where the work of mourning begins. During this stage, institutions support the mourning experience through rituals that help to initiate the recovery process. Family and friends gather together to share the loss and the memory of the loved one in wakes, funerals, and other memorial services. Rituals serve to stop the denial of the loss by helping the survivors begin to face it within group support structures. Family members may even create their own aspects of the ritual, such as my siblings Ruth's and Dave's idea to have the family members shovel dirt onto my mother's casket to help my father accept and deal with the reality of her death. When rituals are not present, for whatever reason, the grief process is often delayed and mourning is extended or interrupted. The "hidden" or less socially accepted losses—such as divorce, abortion, rape, even bankruptcy—which do not have public ritual or social support systems are more difficult to resolve. See "Rituals as a Healing Bridge," p. 180.

The fourth stage is *resolving the loss*. During this stage, the main work of grief goes on intra-psychically. The reality of death is accepted by a process of halting and intermittent steps. The person's thoughts and conversations are occupied with the deceased and his personal experience of his loss. Many times, the person grieving may experience symptoms of pain or others similar to the ones the deceased person had prior to death. This is a process of identification with the loved one and also appeases any guilt related to feelings of aggression.

The fifth and final stage, according to Engel, is *idealization*. This process requires that all negative and hostile feelings toward the deceased be repressed. During this stage, feelings fluctuate between guilt, self-blame for death, sadness, and sense of loss. An almost "perfect" image of the loved one is created in memory, allowing the mourner to experience some of the former pleasures of the relationship. The mourner also takes for himself—consciously and unconsciously—certain admired qualities of the deceased

---

I believe that man will not merely endure: He will prevail. He is immortal, not because he alone among creatures has an inexhaustible voice, but because he has a soul, a spirit capable of compassion and sacrifice and endurance.

— William Faulkner

through the process of identification. If guilt or other negative feelings are present, there is a greater tendency to take on undesirable traits of the deceased or exaggerate the need to fulfill the wishes of the deceased. This process requires a time frame of many months, or even years, as the preoccupation with the deceased progressively lessens, and one turns toward life.

Successful mourning is hard, energy-expending *work*, and it takes a minimum of a year or more. Proof of successful healing is the ability to remember comfortably and realistically both the pleasures and disappointments of the lost relationship or situation. Some of the factors that influence whether the final outcome is positive or negative include the importance of the lost person/object as a source of support (too much dependency hinders outcome); the degree of ambivalence toward the deceased (unresolved, hostile feelings may cause guilt to interfere with resolution); the age of the lost person (a child's death or illness is often harder to deal with); the age of the mourner (the elderly and children may have less capacity to resolve the loss); the number and nature of other relationships; and the number, nature, and frequency of previous grief experiences.

It is important to realize that *all* losses of any type—whether a death, or divorce, or loss of a job, or the more intangible losses such as changes in health status or the death of a cherished hope or dream—follow the process of grieving. It is the *perception* of, or *meaning* given to, an event by the individual affected that identifies it as a loss and triggers the grief reaction. Not all individuals proceed through each step of grief in the same order or with the same intensity. And often a previous step may be revisited as various aspects of a loss are worked through or events reactivate memories that hold emotional power for the grieving individual or group.

★ ★ ★ ★ ★ ★ ★

Dr. Elizabeth Kubler-Ross studied and outlined the five stages of grief in her book *On Death and Dying* while working with dying patients and their families as a psychiatrist in a Chicago hospital in the 1960s. These stages, which can be applied to any loss, are not linear, but rather cyclical:

Stage One: Denial and Isolation. The person thinks or says, "No, not me. This can't be happening. It cannot be true!" There is shock, disbelief, and numbness. We all feel unconsciously that we are immortal or that we are immune from tragedy in our lives or families. Denial functions as a buffer after the unexpected shocking news. It allows a person, family, or community to collect themselves and, with time, mobilize resources and support. Denial is usually a temporary defense and soon is replaced with dawning awareness leading to partial acceptance.

Denial serves as a necessary coping behavior and needs to be respected and not judged even when it creates management problems in dealing with the person or his family. In standing with a dying loved one (or someone facing loss), we need to be aware of the person's strengths and weaknesses, listening and observing to determine how much a person wants to face at a given moment. As a caring friend, we need to allow the person the opportunity to deny the death or loss for as long as needed until he has the resources to face the realities of the loss. See "Strategies to Break Through Denial of Death," p. 184.

Stage Two: Anger (and underlying fear). Feelings of denial are replaced with feelings of rage, envy, resentment, and intense pain. Anger directed outward is very difficult to cope with, for the family and for other support people. People may be very irritable and demanding during this time. Fear may drive their anger toward expression. The person assures himself he is not forgotten by calling attention to himself—even if the behavior is socially unruly and seems excessive. Other people may become targets of the anger because they have what the grieving person has lost and yearns for: good health, a good job, a good marriage. Still others may not overtly express anger, but experience this stage as one of great pain. The grieving person needs to know she is still a valuable human being who is cared for and whose needs will be met in the midst of her distress. See "Seven Steps to Healthy Anger Release," p. 178.

Stage Three: Bargaining. As anger and fear and pain recede, at least temporarily, one hopes for a chance that someone or something will come along and change the situation. The cancer patient hopes for a cure, or an experimental drug that will put the disease in remission. The dying patient wants to live until a certain significant event occurs. Many times, promises are made to God that if He grants this request, then the person will do such and so. It is a magical type of thinking—and part of normal grief and healing.

Stage Four: Depression. This is the stage where anger is turned inward and despair sets in. The person realizes that this situation is not going to magically disappear. The person may wish he had done things differently or feel that he is being justly punished for past misdeeds. He may feel like a martyr or feel sorry for himself. He may mentally "beat himself up," and to him it seems reasonable and logical. He feels abandoned by and different from others. During this phase, people withdraw from support systems and interaction with others.

The person who is dying also withdraws from life and goes inward, a reaction that facilitates the acceptance of all the losses he is experiencing. Reassurances and encouragements are not meaningful for the dying person at this point. Telling him not to be sad is counterproductive. He is sad, appropriately so, for he is saying goodbye to everything and everyone, including his physical life and body. Support people who understand this stage respect his need to express his sorrow and to withdraw from others. Only persons who have worked through the anguish of letting go will progress to the final stage of acceptance.

For a person who is experiencing a loss other than death, there is a reactive depression to the loss. She may give up on life—temporarily. She may withdraw from social interaction. She will have no energy and want to sleep all the time. She may blame herself for her loss and feel like she is a loser, a coward, and a failure. There may be sense of total isolation and deep emptiness inside. Feelings of worthlessness, guilt, and lethargy predominate.

Since depression is such a challenging stage, coping behaviors are essential to activate as quickly as possible. On page 182 is a list of 50 positive coping behaviors that may help someone experiencing great stress or depression. Sensitive support people can also provide loving hope to pull the depressed person through this essential passage.

Stage Five: Acceptance. This stage may arrive temporarily, and then one cycles back through previous stages. Acceptance is a stage where despair recedes, and the grieving person realizes it's time to move forward. She has examined and grieved over the loss; she has found and activated healthy ways to cope; she has discovered meaning and purpose in her loss and in her grief journey; her perceptions about herself and her world have changed; she has redirected her energies and interests to replace previous attachments lost; the darkness of depression has changed to hope and optimism for a new future; she has a positive self identity and feels connected to others and to life.

A dying person has reached a state of peace within himself. He is unafraid of dying and is no longer holding onto anger or regret. He has a sense of trust and forgiveness of himself and others. His faith in God is an anchor and serves as a bridge for coping with the transition from life to death and to life eternal. He will be able to express his feelings of loss, but acceptance for the dying person is void of intense feelings. His struggle is over, and he feels free to let go. He is less talkative, and communication is nonverbal. Death comes as a great relief if the patient is allowed to detach himself slowly from the meaningful relationships in his life. It is the family who usually needs more emotional support now than the patient, as he has found his peace and they are often still struggling with letting him go.

Sue Monk Kidd writes, "To accept the dark night is to accept being human. It is to accept being who I am." A crisis is a holy summons to cross a threshold. It is an ending and a new beginning. It involves leaving behind and stepping forward, a separation and an opportunity. The word *crisis* derives from the Greek words *krisis* and *krino*, which means "a separating." The very root of the word defines our crises as times of severing from old ways and states of being.

Courage comes from the French word *coeur*, which means "heart." To traverse the difficult journey of the dark night of the soul, we have to "take heart." The heart is the seat of the will, the soul. It is the place where our affections and commitments reside. And this is the place where God speaks, where He plants and awakens the new seedling, even as He gently uproots the old. It takes unbelievable courage to let go, to loosen our tight grip on all the things, people, roles, identities, dreams that bind us to the old and familiar.

The opposite of courage is both fear and security. Total security eliminates all risk, and where there is no risk, there is no becoming. Without becoming, there's no genuine life. To be spiritually alive is to reach out and touch the edges of life, as well as the center; to learn to risk and to let go. Perhaps we need to be like children who don clothes to imagine a role. In our journey of personal growth and healing, we need to create for ourselves an imaginary "courage skin" which we can pull on to reach out to new boundaries.

It takes great courage to follow the call to separation, to allow the inner journey to lead us through the process of transformation. It takes courage to change, to confront fears, to break familiar habits. All I can promise is that the internal measurements of joy, vitality, and well being will be the end result if you are faithful to pursuing the transformation of personal growth.

There are three "human technologies" that influence and predict the outcome of crisis and change, whether negative (regression) or positive (growth): 1) having a realistic perception and finding meaning from the change, 2) applying positive coping behaviors, and 3) developing or maintaining adequate social support systems. A lack in any of these three factors will negatively impact the final resolution.

All in the wild March morning I heard the angels call;
It was when the moon was setting and the dark was over all;
The trees began to whisper and the wind began to roll;
And in the wild March morning I heard them call my soul.

— Alfred Lord Tennyson

Attitude and Perception

The mind, through the phenomenon of psycho-neuroimmunology, can heal. Positive, calming thoughts heighten immunity and shift the nervous system into its healing, rest-and-repair mode. The mind-power effect boosts the healing power of effective medicines when patients believe the medicine they are taking will help them. It also works with ineffective medicines through the placebo effect.

Events in life are not the problem. Our thoughts and feelings about events are the problem. It is our attitude that determines whether tough times turn out to be beneficial or whether good times cause one to be miserable. Good health and good fortune can become enemies when they prevent one from doing the work required for personal and spiritual growth. To change requires energy; only *you* can supply the energy to change yourself.

Even when we cannot change our life's circumstances, we can still change our attitude. The psychiatrist Viktor Frankel, who survived the horrors of the Nazi concentration camps, discovered he could control his thoughts. No one could take that freedom from him. His life changed by his awareness, and he lived to teach millions of others the lesson he learned: humans control their own thoughts; only we can choose and change them, and by so doing change our destinies.

Problems are illusions of the material world. Solutions result from immersion in the world of spirit. Wayne Dyer's book *Spiritual Solutions* argues that spiritual problem solving means examining the entire concept of energy in a new way: in the context of vibration and movement. Energy in this context is the speed of an individual's energy field. The higher the frequency, the greater the ability to solve problems. As we increase our frequency and enhance the energy field in our everyday lives, we move into those frequencies he calls spirit. Valerie Hunt, who wrote *Infinite Mind: Science of the Human Vibrations of Consciousness*, describes the healthy human body as a flowing, interactive, electrodynamic energy field. Motion is more natural to life than non-motion—things that keep flowing are inherently good. What interferes with flow will have detrimental effects.

Everything physical, emotional and spiritual is in a state of motion, though it appears solid and motionless. Slow vibrations represent problems: illness, fear, anxiety, stress, depression, ego consciousness, and disharmony. Ordinary human consciousness is slow, but faster than "problems," and is symptom-free. Thought and spirit have faster vibrations. We are spirits who live in physical bodies, not bodies with spirits. Finding God (Spirit) is a coming to one's own true self. Psalm 46:10 says, "Be still and know that I am God." So we can tap into our spiritual resources and find solutions when we are calm (still) and loving.

Thinking through problems and finding solutions is recognizing that we are spirits, and we are connected to the Source (God) always. We walk with God instead of alone; we let go in meditation and prayer and surrender to God. Then we turn our thoughts to love by quietly saying to ourselves: "I seek the highest good for all concerned in this situation here and now." Love becomes a spotlight that dispels darkness. By releasing our own agendas, we are freed from blame, anger, shame, unforgiveness towards ourselves and others.

What we give out—love, generosity, forgiveness, and service—becomes a boomerang: we draw to ourselves those positive spiritual forces. As we grow spiritually in our practices of meditation, prayer, and thankfulness and ask how we can serve or give to the world, we develop spiritual awareness of being connected to God and everyone else. We lose our aloneness. We recognize we have an unlimited inventory of resources available to solve any need or problem we face. At any moment in your life you can ask the Love that surrounds you and connects you to all life to please guide you now. Then release the negative thoughts and self-talk and images and visualize everyone and everything that enters your life as a loving assistant to solve your problems. In these moments, the right person or event arrives to assist you.

In *A Course of Miracles* there is a phrase: "It takes great learning to understand that all things, events, encounters, and circumstances are helpful." It requires possibility thinking, faith, and deep courage to view life this way. What about the worst things we face or observe? Are they truly an opportunity, a seed for a new beginning, a bridge to link us to our best and highest good? We have to change our thinking to realize how divine good or Spirit or God heals and transforms our problems into good. The Infinite has a Plan. . . for each of us. And it is good. We are His/Her Beloved Creation, and growth cycles, whether of flowers and trees or of humans, are always a part of creation.

To change thoughts or intentions that are harmful, begin by filling your mind with thoughts of love, gratitude and forgiveness. Gratitude opens doors to the heart and to life. As we free our minds from negativity, we increase the speed of our invisible energy into a faster frequency that is spiritual. The highest levels of the mind contain capabilities of insight, imagination, creativity, and spiritual

---

Those who bring sunshine to the lives of others cannot keep it from themselves.

— J.M. Barrie

consciousness. The mind moves into higher vibrations as it changes to sound, to light, to spirit. Replacing lower frequencies (negative feelings and thoughts) with the higher frequencies moves us into a space to solve problems.

Imagine your thoughts and inner feelings as flowing energy that you can control because *you are the source!* As you think, so shall you be. Express your *desires* and wishes, and then be willing to *ask*. "Ask and You shall Receive" is the Divine Promise. Go to a quiet place and ask aloud for guidance. Express your *intention* for your desire to be realized and supreme *confidence* that your solution is attainable. Develop a burning *passion*, or a hardening of the will, to do whatever it takes to achieve your desire.

Your thoughts are the energy you act upon. This applies both to what we want *and* what we *don't* want. So we must quit an old habit of thinking about the things we want out of our lives! Focus on health, not disease or symptoms. (My blood pressure is normal and my heart is strong and regular.) Catch your verbalized negative words (listen!), and stop expressing them. Then examine the thought behind the words, and finally, shift to what you want to create instead (your intention).

In an old Native American story of wisdom, a young Indian brave speaks to his tribal chief: "I feel there are two dogs at war within me. One is a white dog and good; the other is black and evil. Who will win this war? What am I to do?"

The chief tells the young brave, "Don't worry. The white dog will win." The brave asks, "Why? How do you know?"

And the chief responds: "Because you will feed him."

So it is with our minds: negative, fearful thoughts take control over our lives only to the extent that we empower them. Whatever we pay attention to grows and expands. If you think about how much you hate being poor, that expands. Shift your thinking and energy from what *is*, to the energy of what you *want*, and what you *intend* to create.

Every time, catch your thoughts and shift to what you *want*, and then *visualize* what you intend to create. Hold the *vision* of what you want—and you will move toward it. You choose: to get what you really want, or what you really don't want. So be mindful of what you think and what you speak.

Focus on God's ability "to provide you with every blessing in abundance." The inexhaustible universe has unlimited abundance: do you visualize a thimble-full or a truck-full? True abundance is an absolute knowing that everything you need will be supplied. Jesus said, "All that I have is yours," in Luke 15:31. Abundance applies to everything: health, wealth, relationships, joy, peace, love, contentment.

★ ★ ★ ★ ★ ★ ★

Sometimes we fantasize that fulfillment will be found elsewhere – in fame, wealth, a new career. We may be surprised to discover that what helps most to transform our lives is the one least explored. Our life's purpose may be hidden in the very place we are standing, in our simple routines of daily life. Sometimes the only way to fulfill our highest potential is by transforming our thoughts. Transforming our lives may mean returning to the same life, yet with a new purpose and meaning.

Rabbi Naomi Levy in *To Begin Again* speaks of the power of a day of rest to find true relaxation from within. A day when we leave materialism and technology behind and enter a world of spirituality, nature, and beauty. A day to live in the sacred present and put worry and cares aside. A day to be truly still—listening to our own inner soul's yearnings, and listening to what the people in our lives are *really* telling us. A day to feel God's presence and all our blessings in our lives.

Rabbi Levy shares the significance of breath—we are a divine creation infused with an eternal spirit. The breath we take is the spirit of God animating us. The Hebrew words for "soul" and "breath" come from the same root. Rabbi Levy offers a breathing meditation as a spiritual, healing discipline:

Take a slow, deep breath in. Feel warmth entering into your being. Breathe out slowly. Imagine yourself releasing all the cares of the week. All tension. All worries. All sadness. Continue to take long, full breaths for several minutes. Each time you inhale, visualize that you are filling up your whole body with lightness, like a helium balloon. With each breath you see yourself slowly floating higher and higher. As you exhale, you see yourself releasing the heavy weight that burdens your soul. Breathe deeply and slowly.

Breathe in peace, breathe out anxiety.
Breathe in light, breathe out darkness.
Breathe in joy, breathe out pain.
Breathe in health, breathe out sickness.
Breathe in trust, breathe out fear.
Breathe in rest, breathe out panic.
Breathe in the life breath that comes from God,
Breathe out all that we take for granted.

And now take a moment to express thanks to God for something you forgot to thank God for today.

If we seek to change our lives and our outcomes, we need to quit feeding our attention and minds with fear, dread, and anxiety. "There is no fear in love, but perfect love casts out fear, because fear involves torment. He who fears has not been made perfect in love" (I John 4:18). What we feed, grows. We need to energize and nourish faith, so fear can be weeded out. Look for tools (tapes, books, movies, TV programs, music, poetry, songs, nature, people) that lift your energy and your spirits and reinforce your tiny seed of faith. A mustard seed is so small it is like a dot

— but Jesus said, "If you have faith like a mustard seed, ...nothing will be impossible for you" (Matthew 17:20). Nourish the tiny specks of faith; water them; give them light and thought and energy — and faith will conquer fear and negativity. Every human will face fears of old age, failure, loneliness, and illness/disease at sometime in her life. Yet our response determines the outcome.

Whenever I feel resentful of the painful struggles inherent in living life, I remind myself how God created beautiful butterflies. They emerge from a chrysalis state and become a butterfly *only* if they go through a process of struggle to pump fluids from their large bodies into the wings. As their bodies shrink, their wings become strong and fluid. We, too, become our divine, true selves ordained by God as we learn our life lessons—often through struggle. Through faith, struggles can become stepping stones to new life. The bigger the challenges and responsibilities one takes on in life, the greater opportunity there is to face and overcome fear.

Growth comes from embracing and exploring the pain and ambiguity of our opposing tensions: good and evil, hope and despair, faith and fear, love and hate, forgiveness and revenge, doing and being, wholeness and fragmentation, positive and negative thinking. This requires courage and choice to not run from them, conceal them, or anesthetize them—but to turn and face the doubts or fears; to take off their masks.

The poet Kahlil Gibran wrote, "Your joy is your sorrow

Your true identity is as a child of God. Once you've claimed it and settled in it, you can find a life of much joy. . . . There is a deep place where your identity resides. Do not let other people run away with your sacred center.

— Henri Nouwen

unmasked. The self-same well from which your laughter rises was oftentimes filled with your tears. . . . The deeper sorrow carves into your being, the more joy you can contain."

To those of you who walk or wait in darkness as you read this book, I want to give you an invitation: Accept life in the places of pain and joy. Gather up the pain and the questions. Hold them gently, respectfully, as a child, upon your lap. Have faith in the movement of your soul to find a way through the pain. Accept the dark. Accept what is. Be true to yourself. Know you are loved and your pain is God's pain. Embrace the chaos and struggles, the splendor and wonder, the agony, the doubts, the fears, the conflicts, the messiness, the ruin and rubble of human misfortune. Remember, light follows darkness; pain can lead to purpose; allow your heart to know that your darkness will become light if you follow your heart path.

Coping Strategies

The following sections describe "healing bridges" that can help you cope with crisis or change in your life. You will also find a list of 50 positive coping strategies and some suggestions for breaking through denial of death or loss. A discussion of stress and how to successfully manage it will aid you in staying physically, mentally, and emotionally healthy even when the winds of change bring turmoil to your life.

Faith and Prayer as a Healing Bridge

Religious faith has long been considered indicative of a positive mental outlook and an overriding sense of personal security. Prayer is a form of meditation, and causes the same helpful, physiological reactions as other forms of meditation. Studies of people with strong religious beliefs have found them to have lower mortality rates, less disability, lower blood pressure (diastolic hypertension), less coronary heart disease, improved immunity, and longer life expectancy after cancer diagnosis.

In an experiment conducted by cardiologist Randolph Byrd at San Francisco General Hospital, prayer was used to influence the medical outcomes of heart disease patients. Three hundred ninety-three patients were divided into two groups. Half were prayed for by other people without the patients' awareness. Those prayed for were five times less likely to require antibiotics and three times less likely to develop pulmonary edema. None required artificial breathing apparatus (versus twelve of those not prayed for), and fewer died. This phenomenon is referred to as distant healing.

Other recent studies strongly indicate the medical efficacy of mind-power healing, including prayer. Dr. Elisabeth Targ, M.D. studied forty AIDS patients and found prayer caused a statistically significant more benign course than control patients. Dr. Larry Dossey, MD, reports in *Healing Words* that of 131 controlled trials conducted, 77 demonstrated statistically significant, positive results. Fifty-six out of the 77 studies yielded outcomes in which the possibility that the results were due to chance was less than one out of one hundred; the remainder yielded outcomes due to chance between two and five out of one hundred.

Dr. Dossey found in examining studies on prayer that the most satisfying results were achieved when people did not pray for a specific outcome, but instead simply let go and got in touch with their highest, most spiritually evolved selves. "They have a quality of acceptance and gratitude, as if things are quite all right in spite of the presence of the disease." This form of surrender expects that whatever happens will be acceptable, versus giving up, which tends to expect the worst and dread it. Such surrender is exemplified by Jesus when He prayed, "Not what I will, but what You will," (Mark 14:36).

★　★　★　★　★　★　★

What is prayer? It is a way to reach out to God; to share our deepest yearnings; to express our secret wishes, hopes, and dreams; to share our unspeakable sins. It connects us to God and forces us to become intimately acquainted with our own souls. Prayer helps us to remember all our hopes—for the world, our loved ones, and ourselves. It gives us strength and courage to express and realize our dreams. It comforts us in times of despair and tragedy.

Prayer leads to action. It is hard to find words to speak our deepest thoughts and feelings to God, and it requires great energy to reach out to God. Yet when we are willing to search for God with all our hearts and souls, and to listen for His voice, God is there, waiting to meet us in prayer. It is a communion of the soul with its Creator, and it leads to action in the world.

Relationships require continuous nurturing. Likewise, prayer and a relationship with God require discipline, honesty, and a deliberate choice to reach out to God. Prayers from the heart can be simple, even wordless; they can be expressed through a song or movements. Prayers require passion, intensity, and openness. Standing naked in the

Great Presence is both frightening and comforting, as we completely lose ourselves in communicating from the depths of our heart, soul, and mind.

There is a famous Jewish prayer, "Master of the Universe." It concludes with these lines:

Into God's hand I entrust my soul,
When I sleep and when I wake.
And with my soul, my body, too;
God is with me, I will not fear.

The Twenty-third Psalm offers a prayer of great comfort, promise, and strength:

The Lord is my Shepherd,
I shall not want.
He makes me to lie down in green pastures.
He leads me beside the still waters.
He restores my soul.
He leads me in the paths of righteousness
    for His name's sake.
Yea, though I walk
    through the Valley of the Shadow of Death,
I will fear no evil,
    for You are with me.
Your rod and Your staff,
    they comfort me.
You prepare a table before me,
    In the presence of my enemies.
You anoint my head with oil;
    My cup runs over.
Surely goodness and mercy shall follow me
    All the days of my life.
And I will dwell in the house of the Lord Forever.

In one Bible story a man comes to Jesus seeking

discipleship; he asks, "Let me first go and bury my father." Jesus responds with tough words: "Follow me, and leave the dead to bury their dead" (Matthew 8:21-22). However, as we look at it in the context of the challenge of personal transformation, we can understand its truth: "leaving the dead" is a call to separating from those things that are deadening, the loyalties that no longer bring us life and vitality. So a crisis is a separation, but also a time of great opportunity. A crisis becomes a time for redirection in our lives and loyalties. So how do we "have" a crisis creatively if we are a person of faith?

There are several spiritual ways to deal with crises events. Most people do one of two things: they reject the crisis and fight against it. Eventually they become cynical and defeated or suffer a loss of faith. These people seek justice. The second way is to say it's God's will and force one's self into an outwardly sweet acceptance, remaining unaffected at the deeper level of the spirit. People who deal with a crisis in this manner seek comfort and peace of mind.

However, there is a third way: the way of waiting. This requires creating a painfully honest and contemplative relationship with one's own depths, with God in the deep center of one's soul. This way is to seek wholeness and transformation. This is the path to soul making.

Theologian Martin Marty wrote, "Brokenness and wounding do not occur in order to break human dignity but to open the heart so God can act." Jesus spoke of entering the "narrow gate" to the inner kingdom of the True

---

We know that to those who love God, who are called according to His plan, everything that happens fits into a pattern for good.

— Romans 8:28

Self. This is the path leading through tight, uncomfortable, heart-wrenching and soul-shaking places that separate one out from the rest of the herd.

Why is faith so critical, so important for survival? First, it gives you a companion: God. In addition, it gives you a belief in yourself that you have the inner strength, resilience, and courage to keep on. It frees you to live life as fully as possible. Faith has no limits: it is a power that transcends our daily challenges. It helps us to see that good can come out of adversity. The eyes of faith see it as God redirecting us, helping us to learn and discover.

Just as pruning is essential to maintain the growth, beauty, and vitality of trees and shrubs, so letting go of both tangible and intangible losses is a form of pruning our lives for greater love, service, and faith—things that last eternally, like the inner spirit. Our problems can become our teachers, healers, and enlighteners, if we open ourselves to embrace their lessons and pain. Tears provide the water of life that leads to growth. Seeds sprout in dark soil—but the innate wisdom within the seed pushes up to the light. The rainbow of colors of our lives is born from light passing through the prism of our pain. Pain released—in writing, in prayer, in sharing with others—opens a space for love to come in. Adversity is a messenger, not a punishment. So ask yourself: How can I turn this event into a Gift of Love—to myself, to others?

"My eyes are my handicap, but my ears are my opportunity," says Ray Charles, musician, singer, and composer. Blind since age seven, he has turned his handicap into a story of triumph and opportunity by focusing on what he has ("music inside me") rather than what he doesn't have (sight). Many of the people whom we look to as heroes or heroines have overcome great losses or life changes. They have turned pain into passion, grief into gifts, hurts into halos, scars into shining stars. Politicians like Abraham Lincoln, Eleanor Roosevelt, and John. F. Kennedy knew tragedy and used it as a spur to greatness. It was Dr. Kubler-Ross who said so eloquently that all the hardships we face in life, which are sometimes viewed as punishments by God, are really *gifts* to us. The gift is the opportunity to grow

Decisions or resolutions made at a time of crisis have great impact, because we are especially vulnerable and therefore more suggestible. These become self-fulfilling prophecies. Therefore, it is critical that we examine and acknowledge how we are thinking so we can create positive rather than negative outcomes and realities for ourselves. Often it is important to delay major decisions until the crisis is past.

To be empowered to change your life you need to accept life's adversities—not deny or avoid them—and also recognize that you are responsible for taking time and space to restore, renew, and prepare yourself to fight for your own life's fullness. And then surrender to the events that brought on the changes and the need to empower yourself. Surrendering means accepting the nature of life, stopping fighting against things you cannot control, and being responsible for doing the right things to restore your life.

In creating Heart Paths for ourselves, we need to follow others who can teach us and help us prevent making costly mistakes when we face life's obstacles. And sometimes it is necessary to forge a new path, one that emerges out of our deep wounds. Our wounds can become gifts for others along our path. There is a phrase in one of Thornton Wilder's stories: "In love's service only the wounded can soldier." Life is difficult. Our hearts must make the choices—for the path to healing, to serving, to creating within our world. The heart hunts the path, and we will know it if we listen to the Still Small Voice Who speaks to each of us regarding the plan. That Voice speaks in both silence—as the prophets heard in the Old Testament—and in the rhythms of living.

As God asked Moses: "What is that in your hand?" Use who you are and what you hold in your hand to live a life of heart-faith and heart-creation. Live with heart-gratitude. Give what you have out of who you are, your being and doing. Forgive yourself and others by focusing on the right questions of life: Why am I here? Why am I alive? What do I need to learn? How can I contribute to life and to others?

———————————

Bring me through darkness into light.
Bring me through pain into peace.
Bring me through death into life.
Be with me, where I go,
And with Everyone I love. In Christ's name I pray.

— Frederick Buechner

Nature as a Healing Bridge

Nature is a great teacher of lessons in living. Have you ever noticed how a tree may grow on a rocky mountainside, or change directions to accommodate an obstacle in its path? Several years ago I saved a rock I liked and put it in a tree between two branches to hold it while I spread pine needles below the tree. I forgot to remove it. This spring I saw it and tried to take it down, but the branches had embraced the stone and made it become a part of itself. Trees teach us how to accept rocks in our lives, absorb the pain, and grow around the problems. Nature teaches us to find our place, grow toward the sunshine, and bypass obstacles. Growth requires changing our responses to the challenges of our lives, moment by moment, if we are to survive. It has always fascinated me to observe how in streams the water flows around rocks or roots or carries leaves lightly on its surface.

I believe God gave us Nature to teach us about the life of the spirit. There is a cycle of life, with Spring, Summer, Fall, and Winter. Each has a unique beauty and strength. Children, like the spring, are fresh and new, budding forth. Winter comes for each of us, but it follows the produce of summer and the brilliant colors of the fall. Each stage gives gifts. And we nurture the growth of life through all stages through love: love of our Creator, love of our natural world, love of each other, love of ourselves, to enable us to be fully, authentically human. It is our Gift back to the Being Who Created All.

Nature changes before our eyes if we have the patience to observe and learn. Nature provides a wonderful gift because it holds our attention, keeping us stimulated at a very sensual level, yet not demanding anything from us. Nature becomes a form of meditation when we walk quietly in it, or watch the ocean's surf, or the clouds move across the sky. As we allow our mind to focus on nature's pictures, voices, and rhythms, our problems, worries, and fears are released. Being in a natural environment is so powerful for relieving the stress of our high-pressure jobs and our inner-city manmade surroundings. Nature opens our hearts and minds. It puts us in touch with our true selves and the source of all life and creation.

Ecopsychologist M.J. Cohen said, "Ninety-five percent or more of the average American's time is spent indoors in artificial and stimulated environments. They may know from TV about global warming and ozone depletion, but they don't know the smell of the spring rain, and the night sounds of the woods." But spending time in nature provides contrasts to the demands of our lives: those who need challenges or risks can find it in activity within nature through hiking or rock climbing or cycling, and focus becomes conquering the natural elements. There is a deep bond of intimacy that unites each of us with all the Creator's creations—plants, animals, and the life forms on earth. The color and vein of a leaf, the soft touch of tender moss, the sounds of a creek flowing over rocks, the earthy smells of forests and swamps—all these teach us about the Creator who loves and cherishes all life. Through nature He restores the earthbound, stressed-out soul during change and loss. Nature is our gift from a loving Creator.

In a number of my stories, contact with the natural world was a significant coping behavior. Some used gardening to calm themselves and release stress. Some sought out special places where they could feel peace and tranquility. Some created beautiful landscapes—either at their homes or in their minds through visualizing a place of peace and security. Even in our cities, there are parks and places of natural beauty. Seek them out. Some people plant window boxes or place pots on a stoop to stay in touch with growing things. Whatever it takes, find a way to experience and respect our connection to life and growth through nature.

Where do you go when the world is too much with you? A garden? A library? A cool stream? On a mountain? Near pounding ocean waves? Everywhere I've lived I've always scouted out a special thinking place — or several. These places renew us and give us comfort. Keep them in reserve . . . when you need a place to ponder or reflect, you'll know exactly where to go.

— RMS

Humor as a Coping Bridge

Humor is a wonderful coping mechanism. The more serious the subject, the more potential it has to be funny. Both guilt and unrealistic expectations may prevent many people from taking themselves more lightly, and you can't have a sense of humor when you feel you have to be perfect. Dr. Walter O'Connell, clinical psychologist, was the founder of "Natural High Therapy"—using humor and poking fun. He says people should take themselves seriously and their egos lightly.

For example, O'Connell was treating a veteran who was very angry, hostile, and potentially disruptive. He named the veteran "The Buddha of Constant Discouragement" and thanked him for giving the other group members an opportunity to practice not being overwhelmed by external hostility. The veteran was faced with a terrible paradox: "Being" the hostile person he was labeled (cooperating with therapist!), or choosing to laugh at himself and letting his hostility be changed, thereby choosing mental health. He eventually chose health.

Honesty with oneself allows one to increase one's use of healthy humor. When we take ourselves lightly by laughing at ourselves, self-esteem increases, stress is reduced, negative patterns are changed, and powerful new perspectives are gained. "Humor has a profound connection with physiological states of the body," writes Raymond A. Moody, Jr., MD in *Laugh After Laugh: The Healing Power of Humor*. Laughter relieves pain, possibly by releasing muscular tension. The brain also is triggered to release catecholamine hormones, which in turn release endorphins, the body's natural painkillers. Additionally, the change of focus may create a temporary anesthetic effect by causing us to focus our attention elsewhere. Laughter also increases longevity: a geriatric medicine physician reported one common characteristic of very healthy elderly patients is a good sense of humor. "He who laughs, lasts."

Persons under stress often use humor as a coping behavior. The more serious and involving the subject, the more potential there is to enjoy jokes about the topic. For example, surgeons and emergency room nurses and personnel may release tension by indulging in black humor. To an outsider this looks like a terrible thing, but it is a way to alleviate the stress from their awesome life-and-death responsibilities. To see humor at times like that requires a kind of dual focus: both the humor and the gravity of the situation.

Other people, like cancer patients, may find ways to use humor to deal with very difficult situations, and in so doing, they are able to bounce back and try again when faced with problems or difficulties. Cancer patients who are pessimistic and apprehensive seem to have more problems with side effects. Humor and camaraderie, however, are very healing forces. Jeannie King, a colon cancer patient, coped with the serious nature of her chemotherapy by creating 18 costumes out of pink tulle. Each time she had chemo, she and two of her best friends created a new outfit to wear. Initially other patients thought they were volunteers who had come to cheer them up—and then were amazed to see Jeannie being hooked up to chemo, too!

There are three focuses of humor: yourself, others, and the situation. People who can laugh at themselves usually demonstrate high self-esteem. People who make fun of or put down others usually have less growth-producing ways of using humor. Humor allows us to change *Ha Ha!* to *A-ha!* We can grow in self-awareness through humor.

Some tips for using humor include:

♥ Select a humorous saying to tell yourself when you are

disappointed: "When life hands me lemons, I'll squeeze them for lemonade!"

♥ Create a signal (like playfully sticking your fingers in your ears and wiggling your fingers) to use within family, work, or peer groups when things need to be lightened up.

♥ Collect and post comical pictures or phrases to see regularly at home or work. Share them with others.

♥ Add humor to the job: a sales manager may call himself the "sales mangler."

♥ Humor accomplishes more than anger. For the chronically late person, say something like, "Thank God you don't run an ambulance service!"

♥ Exaggerate the situation verbally. Often that brings listeners to an awareness of the hidden humor.

♥ Jeannie Robertson, former beauty queen and North Carolina humorist speaker, recommends journaling about your life events and finding ways to change "tragedies" or problem situations into funny tales to share with others.

♥ Collect videos that make you laugh.

♥ Hang around with children. They sometimes see the funny side of things better than adults. They naturally love to laugh and play. Learn from them—or relearn—how to let out the funny child inside you.

♥ Use aikido, the Japanese self-defense, which uses no aggressive moves but turns aside an attacker by gently yet efficiently unbalancing his energy and momentum. Great leaders are often adept at using humor. For example, once while leaving a fancy Manhattan supper club, humorist Robert Bentley turned to the man in uniform at the door and requested, "Would you get us a taxi, please?" The man stiffened. "I'm sorry," he replied coldly, "but I happen to be a rear admiral in the United States Navy." "All right then," said Bentley, "get us a battleship." That is black belt aikido.

Love as a Coping Bridge

Love and health go hand in hand. Researchers from the University of California at Berkeley found that socially isolated people were more susceptible to illness and had death rates about two to three times higher than people whose social lives were richer. Dr. James Lynch, Ph.D., who wrote *The Broken Heart: The Medical Consequences of Loneliness* states that caring is not only moral, but biological and physiological.

A very intriguing study was done by psychologists at Harvard University. People were shown various films (a Nazi war movie, a short film on gardening, and a documentary on Mother Teresa, who earned a Nobel prize for her work with the Sisters of Charity caring for orphans, lepers, poor people and the dying in Calcutta). Measurements were made of a germ-fighting substance in the saliva of people before and after they watched various films. The film on Mother Teresa caused levels of IG-A (an immune agent especially effective in fighting colds and other viruses) to rise sharply, even in nonreligious persons, while no changes occurred in response to other movies.

Loving and being loved causes something deep inside our cells to respond positively. Love sparks healthy biological reactions in much the same way as good food and good fitness. How is this so? Dr. Robert Taylor, a California psychiatrist, attributes it to love's potential to greatly reduce stress. "When people have close relationships, they feel less threatened, less alone, more confident and more in control. Knowing you have people you can turn to in times of need can provide some very important feelings of security, optimism and hope—all of which can be great antidotes to stress."

When people who have had significant losses find new ways to give love—in service or volunteer activities, or in caring for a pet, or in a new "purpose" or life mission—it becomes a bridge to transformation and healing.

Everyone who has lost someone or something she loves dearly faces the challenge of how to rebuild her life "after." I have always felt God calls each of us to accomplish or achieve His plan for our lives—I believe there is a plan if we will listen and seek it. The plan is part of a big picture, and we do not always see or understand the path the plan takes. For me, my path led through many losses over a number of years before I could "see" a new direction and find personal meaning and purpose again. Writing this book and sharing it with you, the reader, became my new purpose and "love" in my life. I hope it makes a big difference for you in your life as you cope with loss and change—however it arrives on your path.

"Love is the total acceptance of another person," says Dr. Gerald Jampolsky, MD, author of *Love is Letting Go of Fear* and founder of the Center for Attitudinal Healing in Tiburon, California. "Love is a relationship without shoulds or shouldn'ts. When we are in love, we accept," says Dr. Ari Kiev, MD, a psychiatrist in New York City and author of *Active Loving*. "In a loving relationship we feel safe and accepted no matter what we do; we feel safe to be ourselves. When someone loves us freely, they have no expectations or demands," says Dr. David Viscott, MD. These psychiatrists say love is acceptance, and the opposite of acceptance is expectation.

Fear or other negative emotions can destroy a relationship if we don't let the other person know what we're feeling. It's important to verbalize feelings; the focus needs to be on *your* feelings, using "I" statements, not "You" statements. Instead of "You hurt me" or "You made me angry," say, "I feel hurt (angry) when you say (or do) that." This form of expression allows the other person to listen and not feel accused or belittled. She appreciates your openness, because it allows her to be open and to share her own vulnerabilities.

Dishonesty or lack of communication is one of the two things that block love. The other is not loving yourself. Only if we love ourselves can we give love to others. The love one has for oneself is the core of all motivation. If you love yourself, you feel worthy. If you feel worthy, you feel competent. If you feel competent, you are able to reach out to others and give love.

To develop self-love, one can start with simple modifications in physical appearance to build self-esteem. Then one needs to address the inner person: one's thoughts. Sometimes one has to wage war on one's negative thoughts. It takes monitoring and awareness of what one is thinking, so that negative patterns can be identified and changed. Eating healthy foods, getting adequate exercise, spending time in nature, praying, meditating, and being 100% present with another are all ways of loving oneself and self-care.

Holding in one's feelings creates a sense of hopelessness and powerlessness, which leads to physical, emotional, and spiritual illness. But people who are loving—accepting of self and others—feel energy and joy and remain healthier. Providing service volunteering in one's community can become a bridge to loving and connecting to others. Doctors have found that elderly patients who engage in volunteer work visit the doctor less often and have fewer complaints. The more connected you are to life, the healthier you are.

Many waters cannot quench love, neither can floods drown it.

— The Song of Solomon

Music as a Coping Bridge

Music has a tremendous power to speak to the human heart. We all know how we are stirred by love songs, patriotic music, or great choral or symphonic renditions. After the terrorist attacks of September 11, 2001, Congress met at the foot of the Capitol and sang "God Bless America," a love song to our country and a prayer for America, in a show of unity. Each night during that fall, Larry King Live ended its hour-long broadcast with a piece of patriotic or inspirational music. Music was very moving and very healing to Americans during this time.

Music can transport us and allow us to be "carried away" by pleasurable sounds; it uplifts us and makes us feel good. Our brains function in four brain wave states: beta, alpha, theta and delta. Beta is a high-speed state the brain maintains as we go about our daily activities. The alpha state is slower and more relaxed. It is a reflecting state, a creative idea and insight state, which allows us to imagine, invent and originate thought. Theta is the dreamlike state we are in just before we drift into sleep or as we awaken, or during deep contemplation or meditation. Delta is the state of deep sleep itself—almost like being in a coma. Music is a valuable tool for coping because it helps us change our brain waves as we shift states: thinking actively when learning or studying, slowing from active to reflective, or entering the meditative state.

The autonomic nervous system slows down while one listens to Baroque music, which has a consistent beat of 55-70 beats per minute, one's pulse rate at rest. Pulse rate automatically slows down to mirror the beat of the music. The music also causes the blood vessels in one's brain to stop contracting, so that more blood is allowed to flow through the brain. This makes one more alert and helps one learn or get creative connections more easily. The brain needs to perceive the music, but this is accomplished when it is not so loud that one "hears" each note.

As music impacts one's physiology, one feels a sense of increased well-being, optimism, and hopefulness. Music is a great stress reducer — it can help people cope with noisy environments, by masking distracting noise.

Baroque music, composed around 1600-1750, is balanced and complete. German composer Johann Sebastian Bach (1695-1750) intuitively knew about balancing alpha and beta states. His music, as well as that of George Friedrich Handel (1685-1759) and an Italian composer, Antonio Vivaldi (1678-1741), shifts between the two brain wave states. Some parts of the music are intense and dramatic and then rapidly shift, becoming slow and calm. Listening to this music gives one a feeling of completeness.

Forgiveness as a Healing Bridge

Many people begin the process of forgiveness in the stage of outrage and anger for the harm done to them. Sometimes people stay stuck here a long time. Or they may learn to express their anger in a healthy way and talk about the pain and hurt they feel, thereby choosing to move beyond anger. Healing begins in the simple act of finding appropriate verbal articulation of the hurt. To swallow the pain without verbalizing it causes dis-ease in our lives and our bodies. Part of forgiveness is feeling the pain and acknowledging our anger. It is important not to build a house around the pain and dwell there. Sharing our pain with God and an appropriate person helps release the suffering and allows the healing process to begin.

A wonderful technique that incorporates the anger and begins the releasing is to pray for the person you are angry with and ask for him to be blessed with health, well-being, and happiness. The key is to *start* the prayer however you need to, and finish it with your prayer for blessings. For example, "If he doesn't get killed in an accident because he deceived me, then, please God, bless and prosper Jim." You may need to pray this for weeks to acknowledge and release your rage or resentment before being able to drop the angry introduction to your prayer. In Psalm 55 and 56, we read some of David's angry prayers. God did not reject or punish David for the anger poured out to Him.

Forgiveness clears the field of weeds so good seeds can grow. The weeds of negativity and condemnation are removed in order to free our hearts and lives from toxic grievances. Often poisonous thoughts begin a little at a time, and this leads to withholding a little love, bit by bit. It destroys our relationships and poisons our heart and soul, and eventually our bodies.

One can practice daily forgiveness by experimenting with easy, *little* resentments. When someone cuts you off while driving and you feel irritation, immediately tell yourself: "I am not going to waste my precious energy in focusing on this. This is not important. Instead, I will think a blessing and focus on peace and calm and breathing life in and resentments out. My mind is calm. My heart is peaceful." Visualize the person you want to be and how you will feel when you've completed your forgiveness work. Not letting rude, offensive behavior or petty acts of an unhappy person damage you is an act of power. Forgiveness shifts our perception to reveal love's presence and power.

In the bigger hurts and resentments, look for ways to get the pain out. Write about it, talk about it, move it out where you can own it and acknowledge it. Ask God to help you create your "story." Ask God to help you re-create yourself, to replace your hurt with forgiveness. Forgiveness means a shift in perception in which we actually come to view a situation or person through eyes of love and compassion. Discord is replaced with peace and harmony. There is no break so great that it cannot be healed, and nothing is impossible with the power of forgiveness. Yet it may take a lifetime to learn to live in freedom, cleared of all hidden resentments and hurts. Resentments taint intentions and drain energy.

★ ★ ★ ★ ★ ★ ★

Our life is like a movie, with thousands of scenes and memories that run in our mind's frames. The very life we're experiencing is a projection of the thoughts we hold. When we hold the energy of thoughts of love and compassion, we see beauty we might otherwise miss. Sometimes frames get scratched or dirty. Wiping the frame clean rewards us with a life of clear vision. We see ourselves more clearly and give compassion to ourselves as well as others. We forgive ourselves. Sometimes the hardest person to forgive is oneself. But when we forgive ourselves, our energy shifts from pain to power.

We need to ask, as we view each memory frame, "Can I forgive this?" If yes, we have learned to accept that life experience. We may never forget a horrible behavior or act perpetrated against us, but we can forgive the person who committed it, and we can accept and integrate the experience as part of our past, so it no longer intrudes and runs our present life. We can practice seeing the other person as a child of God who has forgotten his true self and has acted out of confusion or ignorance. If our answer to the question, "Can I forgive this?" is no, then the frame returns to the memory box to be dealt with again, sometimes from a different angle. We have to come to peace with it in order to move on. Jesus recognized how hard forgiveness is when he said to forgive 70 x 7 times (490).

A daily practice of forgiveness can include, after quieting the mind in prayer or meditation, to ask God's Spirit, "What would you have me forgive today?" Then listen for the still small voice to speak. You may find the person to forgive is yourself: for holding yourself to impossibly high standards of behavior or performance, for ignorance or inadequacies or poor decisions, for unmerciful self-criticisms and punitive self-judgments.

Ask God for help in removing the poison of resentment. At times, sharing with a friend or therapist may help you sort through complicated situations. Experiment until you find techniques that help you forgive with your whole heart: meditation, prayer, writing a letter and burning it, creating a releasing ritual, visualization, or an unorthodox prayer. Empower your life with the fruit of forgiveness.

Seven Steps to Healthy Anger Release
    1. Recognize the anger you're feeling. People often deny

anger out of fear of it or a sense of guilt about having it.

2. Decide what made you angry. Ask yourself: Is this worth getting angry over? Drop small annoyances and forget them.

3. Give the "provider" of your anger the benefit of the doubt. Suggest to yourself a reasonable, justifiable explanation for his behavior.

4. Calm down. Practice some form of mental relaxation. Count to ten. Take five slow, deep breaths. Take a walk to release energy. Then discuss the conflict with less emotion.

5. Make your grievance known without attacking the other person. Focus your complaints or comments non-threateningly by using "I" statements, versus "you." For example, "I feel hurt when you say that..." versus "You are unfair and you are wrong to say that!" "I feel you aren't considering my needs," instead of "You are an inconsiderate jerk!"

6. Listen. Most people don't listen well, especially when angry. Seek to understand the other person's viewpoint. Restate what you heard: "Are you saying you do not think I care about how you feel?" Clarify issues and concerns.

7. Forgive. Forgiveness is the key to happiness and peace of mind. When you forgive someone, you once again experience love, the essence of positive relationships. You remember that you *care* about this person, which may be why their behavior hurt so much in the first place. It also requires you to forgive yourself for your misconception about the person, for judging them, for failing to see them as a loving human being. To forgive yourself releases guilt.

Therefore, if you bring your gift to the altar, and there remembered that your brother has something against you, leave your gift there before the altar, and go your way. First be reconciled to your brother, and then come and offer your gift.

— Matthew 5: 23-24

Rituals as a Healing Bridge

Another powerful tool for coping with any loss or change is healing rituals. Societies and cultures around the world build memorials in an effort to heal from social traumas, whether for thousands lost in a war, such as the Vietnam Veterans Memorial, or for one who meant so much to so many, such as John Kennedy's Eternal Flame, or impromptu flowers, crosses, and ribbons placed along a roadside where someone died in an accident. The memorial has power to evoke many of our feelings about the trauma. The location of a memorial—whether a grave, a religious structure, or a monument or symbol—becomes sacred to us as we imbue it with a special meaning and purpose.

A specific place assists the grieving process by focusing grief and providing an opportunity to share it with others. Communication and behavior at these special places are prescribed by ritual and help us express difficult emotions.

Some of the key elements of rituals include:

♥ Healing rituals always involve symbolism. Intangibles can be represented by symbolic items: patriotism and service from a folded flag and gun salute; a pin to represent group membership; a wedding ring to symbolize commitment or joining lives.

♥ Preparing for the ritual is part of the ritual process. Preparation adds power and focus and helps prepare us mentally for the ceremony or event.

♥ Everyone should be involved both in preparing and in enacting the ritual.

♥ Choosing the setting for the ritual is important. It must be meaningful and appropriate to all who participate.

♥   Rituals of Transformation are rarely easy, because they involve helping people change their self-image. Eagle Scouts know how much focus and energy are required to reach that goal. It is an investment of oneself. Outward Bound programs or a ropes course is designed to require preparation and commitment for transformation.

♥   Experts are often utilized. Clergy or judges perform marriages, and clergy may officiate at funerals. Sometimes families create their own rituals, such as scattering ashes or planting a tree in memory of a loved one.

It is important to consider your family's style of dealing with traumatization. Each family has established patterns of expressing (or avoiding) feelings. You can create family or group rituals to heal traumatization. First, identify the specific trauma and its effects on each person. Then think of what symbols would be useful to remind the family members of (1) the loss, (2) what has changed, and (3) the idea of transition and transformation. And finally plan and implement the ritual as a bridge to completion of the past and a doorway to a new phase of life.

Lord, still the clamor of our days,
And calm our rushing, anxious ways;
In silence teach us how to praise;
Give us peace within your love. . . .

— B.J. Hoff

50 Positive Coping Behaviors

1. Meditation
2. Prayer
3. Solitude
4. Silence
5. Holy leisure
6. Simplicity
7. Eucharist/Communion
8. Reading the Bible or Holy Books
9. Reading inspirational, motivational literature
10. Balanced nutrition, diet rich in plant-based foods
11. Taking food supplements
12. Exercise, Stretching
13. Sports
14. Hiking
15. Riding a bike
16. Massage
17. Yoga
18. Adequate rest and relaxation
19. Change of scenery or environment
20. Rituals that touch the space of mystery and transformation
21. Deep encounters with nature and creation
22. Driving in the mountains
23. Growing things
24. Gardening
25. Expressing oneself creatively
26. Hobbies
27. Collecting symbols and images (e.g. rainbow, butterfly, rosary, candlesticks, cross)
28. Listening to music

29. Singing
30. Playing an instrument
31. Art—painting and drawing
32. Play
33. Laughter and humor
34. Playing with children
35. Playing with pets
36. Journaling
37. Writing letters to self or deceased person
38. Writing down goals
39. Finding a new goal or purpose
40. Discovering purpose and meaning
41. Gratitude, thankfulness, blessing life
42. Seeking positive relationships for sharing and caring
43. Service and loving kindness
44. Talking to oneself—externalizing inner thoughts
45. Creating affirmations (positive self-talk)
46. Using visualizations, e.g. How you want your life to be, Changes you will make, Describe your ideal day or ideal relationship, Create images of forgiveness.
47. Screaming, Crying, Weeping
48. Beating a pillow or mattress to release stored anger
49. Breaking eggs in a forest or wooded area to release anger
50. Practicing forgiveness (self and others)

Actions to Break Through Denial of Death

1. Face death openly; begin by taking actions, like planning or reviewing legal or financial documents.
2. Read books on death and dying. Attend seminars.
3. Discuss death openly with loved ones.
4. Be aware of your own reactions, feelings, thoughts, fears, and aversions.
5. Talk with someone dying, or someone with a recent loss.
6. Talk with professionals about your questions: hospital personnel, physicians, hospice personnel, morticians.
7. Take responsibility for writing a will.
8. Prepare belongings and important papers for the eventuality of your demise.
9. Discuss preferences for funeral, burial, cremation, donation of body parts, etc. Complete a Living Will, a document that requests your life not be prolonged by artificial means.
10. Let your family lawyer know the location of important papers, safe-deposit boxes, insurance policies, and other personal and financial information.
11. Examine the words used to refer to death in our culture, which are often euphemisms rather than direct and factual. Which of these words do you find difficult? Dead, dying, gone, death, expired, lost, absent, passed away, deceased, passed over, gone to sleep, gone to eternal rest, finished, buried, cremated, murdered, abandoned, grieving, mourning, went to heaven, God called him home, (add any other words you hear or use).
12. When words are difficult to find to discuss death, drawing can be a valuable therapeutic tool for both children and adults. Draw a personal experience, or your ideas of

what death is, or how you experience loss. After you finish, study it. What does it say to you? What can you learn about yourself? Share it with a friend or loved one.

13. Writing Exercises:

A. Write or sit and think about: If I had six months to live I would... How would you spend your time? What is important? Who do you want to be with? Are there things you would *not* do? This identifies your values.

B. Make a specific list of items you want to give to someone else after you die. What is most important to you? Whom do you want to give to?

C. Write your eulogy or obituary. What do you want remembered about your life? Will anything be missing from your life that you need to add to your life *now*? Do something to incorporate your dreams and goals *now*.

D. Choose your tombstone epitaph.

Remember that all these exercises are to help you face the reality of your death so that *today* you can live more fully, make changes when necessary or desirable, take care of unfinished business quickly, and spend your precious time doing the essential, the meaningful, and the joyful.

You can just as easily laugh and play while you grow as become serious and overwhelmed.

— Gary Zukav

Understanding and Coping with Stress

Stress is an unavoidable part of life. We all need some stress to motivate us to satisfy our needs. When there is too little, there is no motivation for growth and change; too much, and we begin to close down and get overwhelmed. So it's good to learn your optimal level of stress and then do the necessary things to keep your stress level in balance.

Excessive production of stress hormones such as adrenaline or cortisol can cause physiological changes such as stunted growth, high blood pressure, ulcers and canker sores, bone loss, weakened muscles, weakened immune system, depression, memory loss, and increased insulin levels (leading to higher fat deposits). The connection between stress and heart disease has not been scientifically proven. But a person who has heart disease may increase the risk of a heart attack depending on his or her body's reaction to stressful events. Stress also triggers the fight or flight hormones like cortisol, epinephrine, and norepinephrine produced by the adrenal glands. Heart rate and blood pressure are raised, as well as levels of blood sugar, which may cause damage to coronary arterial linings.

The good news is that you can do something about stress. Effective planning can help keep stress from overwhelming you. Develop awareness of your body and how it reacts, so you can learn to cope by knowing exactly what is causing you excessive stress and creating solutions to the causes. A stress management course may be valuable, as may talking with a therapist who can teach you relaxation techniques as well as help you identify precipitating factors. Journaling may also increase self-awareness.

Most people do not realize even happy events like graduations, weddings, family reunions, promotions or recogni-
tions, or a new baby create stress in our lives. These positive events often bring a whole new set of decisions, choices,
adjustments, and worries to handle. So your response to
change, how you relate to the world around you, and your
perception about the situation are key issues.

You should also evaluate your job to see if you are well-
fitted for the type or degree of stress inherent in that career choice. Life and death situations faced in professions
such as medicine, law enforcement, and firefighting are
innately stress-oriented. Some people thrive on crisis response, while others find it debilitating.

In the 1980s, psychologist Suzanne Ouellette Kobasa,
Ph.D., led studies at the University of Chicago to see how
and when people survived relentless stress. She found that
survivors share three specific personality traits that appear to afford them a high degree of stress resistance: they
are committed to what they do; they feel in control of their
lives; and they see change as a challenge rather than a
threat. This hardiness viewpoint accounts for human resilience, initiative, and creativity. It helps explain how leaders such as Winston Churchill, Franklin D. Roosevelt, and
Dwight D. Eisenhower got the world (and themselves)
through a terrible war, and Mayor Giuliani helped New York
City and the United States face and deal with the horrific
events of 9/11/01.

★ ★ ★ ★ ★ ★ ★

Psychologists Robert Kriegel, Ph.D., and Marilyn Harris Kriegel Ph.D. contributed to our understanding of how
people can have peak performance under pressure in a
book entitled *The C Zone*. They found that Type C's, who
perform at their peak under pressure, choose behaviors
from both driven, aggressive type A's and patient, passive

Type B's to fit their needs and situation. These Type C peak performers demonstrate three consistent characteristics: commitment, confidence, and control.

To perform at this level requires a combination of specific attitudes and skills. Skill implies a thorough knowledge of whatever game/job/role you are playing; the ability to develop game-winning strategies that capitalize on your strengths; and a competence or expertise in the execution phase. Attitude includes all of our "inner" or mental processes, many of which are unconscious. Attitude is the key to peak performance. In sports, in life, and among high-powered executives, the most significant factor that distinguished top from moderate performers was attitude.

The ability to perform as a Type C—one who is committed, confident, and in control—is innate in everyone. Often humans, when forced to give up control over their lives or things that have made them feel secure, will react with anger and hostility. Anger mobilizes energy. It is "fire in the belly" to create action and movement. The anger lessens when a person finds coping strategies to bring some measure of control back into his life. Sometimes, when there is no way to "be in control" over the situation or if it involves other people, the person finds surrendering to God and a plan bigger than himself provides release and healing.

The following scale was developed by researchers at the University of Washington School of Medicine to rank stressful events (positive and negative) in a person's life. The higher the total score accumulated in the preceding year, the more likely there will be a serious illness in the immediate future. The purpose of counting stressor points is to allow one to problem-solve and make wise choices about self-care.

Thomas H. Holms & Richard H. Rahe's Stress Rating Scale*

Event	Value	Event	Value
Death of a spouse	100	Child leaving home	29
Divorce	73	Trouble with in-laws	29
Marital separation	65	Personal achievement	28
Jail term	63	Spouse begins/stops work	26
Death of close family member	63	Starting/finishing school	26
Personal illness or injury	53	Change in living conditions	25
Marriage	50	Revision of personal habits	24
Fired from work	47	Trouble with boss	23
Marital reconciliation	45	Change in work conditions	20
Retirement	45	Change in residence	20
Change family member's health	44	Change in schools	20
Pregnancy	40	Change recreational habits	19
Sexual difficulties	39	Change in church activities	19
Addition to family	39	Change in social activities	18
Business readjustment	39	Loan under $10,000	17
Change in financial status	38	Change in sleeping habits	16
Death of a close friend	37	Change family gatherings	15
Change to different line of work	36	Change in eating habits	15
Change in marital arguments	36	Vacation	13
Mortgage or loan over $10,000	31	Christmas season	12
Foreclosure of mortgage/loan	30	Traffic ticket	11
Change in work responsibilities	29		

* *Journal of Psychosomatic Research*, Volume 11, T.H. Holms and R.H. Rahe, "The Social Readjustment Rating Scale," 1967, Pergamon Press, Ltd.

50-100	Mild stress
101-199	Moderate stress. Increased chance of illness.
Over 200	High stress. 80% chance of developing a serious, stress-related illness in the future (18-24 months).

Everyone needs to find ways to relieve stress that work for him. There is no one right solution for everyone. Try some of the suggestions in the list of 50 Positive Coping Strategies," pages 182-183. A combination of strategies—including physical, mental, social, and spiritual—is useful for best results.

Staying healthy is a key factor in stress management. Americans are not getting adequate nutrition for numerous reasons, including fast-paced lives, the advertising and convenience of fast foods, and the ready availability of packaged, low-nutrient, high-simple carbohydrate, high-fat foods. According to Dr. Steve Chaney, a cancer researcher and professor at the University of North Carolina at Chapel Hill, the incidence of obesity and type 2 diabetes has increased 70% in the past 10 years in the 30-40 age group and has doubled in children. Obesity and diabetes increase the risk of heart attack, stroke, nerve damage, blindness, and poor circulation leading to amputations. Coronary heart disease, cancer, and osteoporosis are all linked to inadequate intake of several vitamins.

Eating a diet rich in fresh fruits and vegetables, balanced with whole grains and low-fat sources of protein such as soy, tofu, fish, and range-fed chicken, will reduce the body's need to cope with chemicals and additives, so as to detoxify and nourish the cells. Another important factor is to drink eight or more glasses of pure water every day to purify the body, maintain hydration, and remove toxins. During high stress, the body requires increased nutritional support with nutrients like Vitamins C, E, the 8 essential B's, zinc, and additional protein. By eating wisely and well (minimum of 2-3 fresh fruit and 3-5 fresh vegetables daily) and taking food-based supplements for extra nutrients, we add health and wellness insurance for high-stress times. If you don't take care of your body, where will you live?

Sugar, coffee, alcohol, and chemical additives in manufactured foods are especially harmful when one needs to reduce the physiological effects of stress. Chocolate, on the other hand, releases brain hormones that create a positive euphoria. Breads, pasta, rice, cereals, potatoes, and chocolate promote drowsiness. However, binge eating or excessive intake of calories turns to fat, causing weight problems and leading to more stress.

The Ladder of Health (a way to visualize the Health-Illness Continuum)

Optimum Health	Reach this level for high-level wellness.
Nutrition Program	Begin a Guaranteed Health Program
++ Become Aware	Become aware of what can happen & what is possible for our health.
Neutral Zone**	The majority of persons spend a part of their lives here
— Symptoms & Illness	If we don't climb the ladder, we go down…
Disease	When we reach this level, we may never recover
Dr.'s Care	Essential
Death	It all ends here!

**From the Neutral Zone, it is either up or down the ladder (the choice is up to you)

To move up the Ladder of Optimal Health we need to follow these steps: (1) Gain awareness of what can happen and what is possible to make healthier changes; (2) Begin a guaranteed health program consisting of a healthier, plant-based diet, quality food supplementation products, consistent exercise, and balanced mental/spiritual practices, and (3) Discover what is *your* optimal health.

Unless we actively choose health by taking positive action, we will begin to move from the Neutral Zone downward on the Health Ladder. We will begin to develop symptoms of "dis-ease." Initially they will be minor, but if we fail to pay attention, those symptoms will increase in severity. A cold becomes a chronic sinus infection. Fatigue becomes Chronic Fatigue Syndrome. Here is where most people seek medical attention from their doctors to "fix" the symptoms or disease. If unhealthy patterns and practices are not changed, the person with an illness will begin a slide towards premature death, in spite of the best medical care available in the world today.

Stress Warning Signs
- Loss of energy; unusual fatigue
- Feeling out of control
- Exhibiting uncharacteristic emotions and actions; crying unexpectedly
- Loss of interest in people and activities you once found pleasurable
- Isolation, withdrawal from others
- Overuse of alcohol, sleeping pills, caffeine, or cigarettes
- Increased health problems
- Change in appetite
- Loss of memory, forgetfulness
- Lack of concentration
- Irritability or impatience
- Suicidal thoughts
- Anxiety/panic attacks, worry
- Distractibility

Tips for Managing Stress
- ♥ Set limits for yourself: Define what you can, can't, won't, will do
- ♥ Have realistic expectations of yourself and others
- ♥ Set realistic goals: sometimes they need to be short term in focus (daily); write them down.
- ♥ Ask for help and accept it. Reach out for support.
- ♥ Take care of yourself. Respect your limits; focus on basic needs: food, water, sleep, exercise, lifestyle balance, personal care.
- ♥ Say No, guilt free
- ♥ Release; forgive
- ♥ Find humor; laugh
- ♥ Express feelings (verbally; journal; cry; scream)

♥ Practice your faith (prayer, gratitude/thanksgiving journal)

♥ Assert yourself: You do not have to meet other's expectations or demands. It's okay to say no, or "I need to think about that first."

♥ Stop smoking, drinking. Nicotine acts as a stimulant and creates more physical stress symptoms. Give yourself a gift by dropping unhealthy habits.

♥ Stop over-spending. Cut up the credit cards or put them in your safe deposit box.

♥ Exercise regularly. Even 10 minutes first thing in the morning is a wonderful way to begin the day. Aerobic exercise has been shown to release endorphins, natural brain chemicals that help you feel happier, maintain a positive attitude, and sleep better at night. Participate in non competitive exercise: walking, yoga, cycling.

♥ Take responsibility for controlling what you can and leaving behind what you cannot control. Try to avoid numerous major changes simultaneously.

♥ Relax every day. Study and practice relaxation methods. Combine opposites: a time for deep relaxation and a time for aerobic exercise protects your body from the effects of stress.

♥ Evaluate and reduce stress factors. Simplify your life. Take time out to plan and prioritize based on your values and goals. Learn time management skills.

♥ Examine your values and live your life based on them. When your actions reflect your beliefs, you feel better no matter how busy your life is. *The Seven Habits of Highly Effective People* by Dr. Steven Covey and *Even Eagles Need a Push* by David McNally are wonderful resources for clarifying personal values and goals; also, Bob Proctor's *You Were Born Rich.*

♥ We can balance our lives by looking at seven areas as a Wheel of Life: Where are you now (from 0% on a continuum) in terms of where you want to be (as 100%)? If you have a 'flat tire," you can create small steps (a goal) in an area to increase and benefit other areas of your life. You can prioritize the seven areas by ranking which is most important right now to make changes in to balance or improve your life. These areas may and should shift over time to "balance" your Wheel of Life. The seven areas are: Career, Family, Physical, Social, Mental, Spiritual, Financial.

♥ Sell yourself to yourself. When you feel overwhelmed or like a failure, it is important to recall your previous successes, no matter how tiny or seemingly insignificant. Write down your successes in a special book (for your eyes only).

♥ Be grateful. Thankfulness for all our blessings increases inner happiness and joy. List "gratitudes" daily and give thanks to the Creator of Life. Even in the midst of stress or grief, we can find small (yet precious) things to be grateful for: the sunshine, the rain, the beauty of a flower or tree, the wonder of a bird on the wing, a rainbow, the smile of a child, or a hug, the ability to walk or breathe or see.

Specific Techniques:

♥ Deep breathing exercises (Breathe in so stomach expands, slowly release breath to count: 5 in, 5 out)

♥ Meditations (calming and focusing the mind on a word or sound or object)

♥ Progressive muscle relaxation (tighten and release muscles)

♥ Mental imagery relaxation (visualize a special place)

♥ Relaxation to music

♥ Biofeedback – Biofeedback helps a person learn stress-reduction skills by using various instruments to measure temperature, heart rate, muscle tension, and other vital signs as a person attempts to relax. The goal of biofeedback is to teach you to monitor your own body as you relax. It is used to gain control over certain bodily functions that cause tension and physical pain. For example, if a headache develops slowly, some people can use biofeedback to stop the process before it becomes full blown.

♥ Promote sleep. Establish a regular sleep schedule. Go to bed and get up at the same time daily. Make sure your bed and surroundings are relaxing and comfortable. Keep your bedroom dark and quiet. Use your bed only to sleep (not watch TV or work). Avoid napping too much during the day. Talk out or write out to release worries. Listen to relaxing music. If you can't sleep, get up and do something relaxing until tired. Avoid caffeine and excessive fluids too close to bedtime. Exercise at least 2-3 hours before bedtime so you aren't over-stimulated.

Definitions

Stress: any external stimulus, from threatening words to the sound of a gunshot, that the brain interprets as dangerous

Fear: the short term physiological response produced by both the brain and the body in response to danger.

Anxiety: a sense or apprehension that shares many of the same symptoms as fear but builds more slowly and lingers longer.

Depression: prolonged sadness that results in a blunting of emotions and a sense of futility, often more serious when accompanied by an anxiety disorder.

No vision and you perish;
No ideal and you're lost;
Your heart must ever cherish
    Some faith at any cost.
Some hope, some dream to cling to,
Some rainbow in the sky,
Some melody to cling to,
    Some service that is high.

        — Harriet Du Qutermont

Post Traumatic Stress Disorder

Everyone at some time or another encounters trauma in the course of living. Trauma does exert a profound effect on our lives, temporarily destroying our sense of being in control. For some people, the negative effects linger on long after the initial event. Sometimes multiple, rapid changes or losses prevent adequate integration time. Some people turn to negative coping methods to deal with the pain or trauma, such as alcohol, nicotine, or drug abuse; sexual or physical abuse of others; violence; gambling; risk-taking; overeating; suicide; homicide; or simply a retreat from living.

There is a difference between *trauma* and *traumatization*. Everyone experiences trauma, but not all are traumatized. People are traumatized when the effects of a trauma continue to disrupt or control their lives, even though the effects may be buried for years before they emerge. PTSD is a more severe form of traumatization. Five factors determine whether you'll be traumatized by an event. Three relate to how you *experience* the event: the meaning you give it, your personal characteristics, and the actual nature of the event. Two others relate to how you *cope* with the event: your personal coping skills and the kind of help you get from other people.

The common denominator of psychological trauma is a feeling of "intense fear, helplessness, loss of control, and threat of annihilation," according to the *Comprehensive Textbook of Psychiatry*. The many symptoms of post-traumatic stress disorder fall into three main categories: "hyper arousal," "intrusion," and "constriction." Hyper arousal reflects the persistent expectation of danger; intrusion applies to the indelible imprint of the traumatic moment; constriction relates to the numbing response of surrender.

Often Post Traumatic Stress Disorder is associated with war veterans. In fact, the term came into more common use in the past twenty years, after the Vietnam War. The diagnosis of PTSD was only developed a decade ago. But the feeling of being different from other people is common to anyone who has experienced traumas related to wars, violent crime, physical and sexual abuse, life in an alcoholic family, accidents and disasters (both manmade and natural), and chronic and terminal illnesses. Even if we have been on the periphery of events, we are affected by massive trauma.

The psycho-physiological changes of post-traumatic stress disorder are both extensive and enduring. Many people experienced startle reactions, hyper alertness, nightmares, and psychosomatic complaints after the terrorist attacks of September 11. These symptoms relate to chronic arousal of the autonomic nervous system. Irritability and explosively aggressive behavior reflect a shattered and disorganized fight-or-flight response to overwhelming danger. The sympathetic nervous system may be continually in overdrive, with high anxiety and physiological preparedness evident, which is maladaptive when chronic. Post-traumatic stress also affects sleep, delaying ability to fall asleep quickly and creating more frequent awakening during the night.

Secondly, long after the danger is past, traumatized people relieve the event as though it were continually recurring in the present. Time stops at the moment of trauma. It becomes a repetitive intrusion into the survivor's life as a frozen, wordless traumatic memory with vivid sensations and images. The central nervous system may become altered when high levels of adrenaline and other stress hormones are circulating at the time of the event. Deep imprints on memory traces are established, and linguistic encoding is inactivated.

Children may reenact traumatic scenes literally in their play, with a grim and monotonous tone. Adults may reenact the trauma scene in a disguised form, sometimes dangerously (such as putting themselves into situations that jeopardize safety) and sometimes in a socially useful manner (like volunteering as a rape crisis counselor). The repetitiveness is an attempt to heal the trauma. Traumas are resolved when the survivor develops a new mental "schema" (paradigm) for understanding what happened. However, because reliving the traumatic experience provokes such intense emotional distress, traumatized people go to great lengths to avoid it. This leads to a narrowing of consciousness, a withdrawal from engagement with others, and an impoverished life.

Numbing is the third cardinal symptom of post-traumatic stress disorder. The helpless person alters her state of consciousness to escape the situation. This is nature's way to protect against unbearable pain. Both terror and rage may occur as well as, paradoxically, a state of detached calm, in which terror, rage, and pain dissolve. Perceptions and time are altered. The person is emotionally detached and may observe the event as if from outside his body. Voluntary action is surrendered, critical judgment is suspended, perceptions are heightened, and sensations are altered, resulting in numbness and analgesia. It is like a hypnotic trance; traumatic events serve as powerful activators of the capacity for trance, which is a normal property of human consciousness.

In an acute trauma state, pain perception is reduced. It is entered without conscious choice when traumatized. Drug and alcohol use also create a numbing effect like that of traumatic hypnosis, which explains why so many war veterans and traumatized persons have used alcohol or drugs—to ease the pain. However, this becomes mal-adaptive, because traumas are walled off and integration of the experience necessary for healing is prevented. The tragedy is that fear rules their lives, and traumatized people deprive themselves of new opportunities for successful coping that might mitigate the effect of the traumatic experience.

Dr. Judith Herman, MD, reported in *Trauma and Recovery* that dissociation lies at the heart of traumatic stress disorders, and that the people most likely to develop long-lasting PTSD are those survivors of disasters, terrorist attacks, and combat who entered a dissociative state at the time of the traumatic event. Formerly viewed as a creative defense to overwhelming terror, it is possible this mental escape necessary at the time may be purchased at far too great a price, including self-destructive attacks on their own bodies and persistent somatic symptoms for which no physical cause can be identified. These traumatized people relive in their bodies moments of terror they are unable to describe in words. Dissociation is a mechanism that allows intense sensory and emotional experiences to disconnect from the sensory domain of language and memory, and internally silences terrorized people.

★ ★ ★ ★ ★ ★ ★

Families and friends also suffer from the emotional withdrawal of the traumatized person, who feels no one understands. However, recovery depends on the empowerment of the survivor and the creation of new connections. Recovery occurs only in relationships, not in isolation. Damaged capabilities must be restored: trust, autonomy, initiative, competence, identity and intimacy. Just as in childhood we form relationships with our parents for healthy growth, so must re-formed relationships be the central focus for healing and renewal.

The first principle is empowerment of the survivor, who must choose to be the author and arbiter of his own recovery. Control is restored to the traumatized person; personal power to act and decide on one's own behalf is essential. Psychotherapy can become a valuable tool because the sole purpose is to promote the recovery of the patient. The therapist becomes an ally, placing all her resources of knowledge, skill and experience at the person's disposal. The therapist respects the client's autonomy and assists him to clearly define how he wants to think, feel, and act as a result of recovery, and commits to a collaborative partnership to reach that goal. The therapist stands *with* the person, bearing witness to the pain and horrors, and in this role fosters insight and empathic connection, providing intellectual and relational tools for recovery. The therapeutic relationship serves as a bridge between rebuilding the inner world of the survivor and reconnecting with the outer world of his life.

Because therapists enter into the anguish and despair of their clients, they need adequate support systems outside their professional role so they are not overwhelmed by their feelings and lose their ability to keep the promise to bear witness. "Witness guilt"—similar to clients' "survivor guilt"—may be a problem as well. People sometimes feel guilty for being spared the suffering that the patient has endured, which can lead to difficulty in enjoying the ordinary pleasures of one's own life.

Sometimes a friend or family member may play the role of "therapist" for a traumatized person, but results will be better with a licensed psychotherapist. Until the victim

---

You gain strength, courage, and confidence by every experience in which you really stop to look fear in the face. You must do the things which you think you cannot do.

— Eleanor Roosevelt

chooses to seek this relationship, however, the stand-in "therapist" must pay attention to his own self-care to prevent burnout. He must not take on too much personal responsibility for his friend or family member's life. Careful attention to boundaries of the relationship, whether with a therapist or friend, is essential. Boundaries provide a safe arena for recovery work and benefit both therapist and client with clearly defined ground rules.

Recovery unfolds in three stages. First, establishment of safety must be achieved. The second stage is characterized by remembering, mourning, and resolving the trauma and losses. In the third stage one learns to reconnect with ordinary life.

Safety starts with building a therapeutic relationship, concurrently with taking control of the body's basic needs: establishing normal sleep, following a healthy diet, exercising, controlling self-destructive behaviors, managing of post-traumatic symptoms. It then extends into the environment: establishing a safe living situation, financial security, mobility, and a plan for self-protection that encompasses the client's daily life, including social support. The goal is to reduce the hyper arousal and intrusive symptoms and to increase the client's self-empowerment, as well as to mobilize caring people and develop a plan for future protection and self-care.

Creating a safe environment can lead to major changes in a life, with difficult choices and sacrifices. Without freedom, there can be no safety and no recovery, yet freedom (emotional, social, financial, familial, political, etc.) is often achieved at great cost. In order to gain freedom, survivors may have to give up almost everything else. Battered women may lose homes, friends, and livelihood. Survivors of childhood abuse may lose their families. Political refugees may lose their homes and homeland. This type of sacrifice is rarely fully appreciated by others.

Remembering and mourning is a time for telling the story in complete detail. The client gets to speak the unspeakable while the therapist serves as a witness and ally. This stage requires great courage to uncover the trauma of the past and integrate the experience into the present so that the client's future has value and meaning. Safety is always preserved and balanced constantly against the need to face the past. Together, client and therapist learn to negotiate a safe passage between the towering mountains of constriction and intrusion. The goal is to prevent stagnation in recovery, yet not overwhelm the client with fruitless reliving of the trauma. During this time of "uncovering" work, the client will not function at his highest level of ability, so he needs to be gentle with himself. This work many times can be done within the normal social framework of a person's life, although occasionally hospital protection is required. This should not be attempted when a client is facing immediate life crises or pursuing important goals.

During this phase, a client reviews his life prior to the trauma, re-creates the flow of his life, and restores a sense of continuity between past and present. Important relationships, ideals and dreams, and prior struggles or conflicts are valuable to assess. This context of a person's life helps establish the particular meaning the trauma had for the client.

Memories—usually fragmented components of frozen imagery and sensation—need to be reconstructed in an organized, detailed, and verbal account, oriented in time and historical context. The event, the client's response to it, and the responses of the important people in her life are all part of the picture, described in vivid words and sensations (what they see, hear, smell, feel, and think). These memories and sensations—such as certain smells, racing heart, muscle tension, weakness in legs, inability to scream or speak or act—are often avoided, disassociated, or partially described because they are so aversive. Both children and adults may need to draw or paint or write a letter or poem to re-create the memories and perceptions. Facts without the accompanying emotions are sterile and produce no results. The therapist provides a sense of safe connection and a protected anchorage while the client re-experiences the feelings in all their intensity so that the mind and emotions can establish meaning and answer for themselves the unfathomable questions: Why? and Why me? Values and beliefs are reconstructed, issues of guilt and responsibility are addressed, and what action to take as a remedy for injustice is decided.

As she rebuilds her own shattered assumptions about meaning, order, justice, security, and morality in the world, the client may come in conflict with beliefs held by important people in her life. The client struggles to restore her own sense of worth, while preparing to sustain it when facing critical judgments of others. Therefore, the therapist carries a huge responsibility: to provide a context that is cognitive, emotional, and moral. The therapist normalizes the client's responses, facilitates naming and use of language, shares the emotional burden of the trauma, and helps construct a new interpretation of the traumatic experience that affirms the dignity and value of the survivor. This requires enormous patience and a belief in the restorative power of truth telling through psychotherapeutic work. The goal of telling the traumatic story is integration and transformation. The trauma story becomes a testimony. The new story is no longer about shame and humiliation, but about dignity and virtue. Universally, testimony is a ritual of healing, with both a private dimension—confessional and spiritual—and a public dimension—political and judicial. The story is treated with formality and solemnity, allowing clients to regain the world they have lost.

It has been found that the action of telling a story in the safety of a protected relationship actually can produce a change in the abnormal processing of the traumatic memory; and with the memory transformation, many of the major symptoms of post-traumatic stress disorder are relieved. However, the constrictive symptoms of numbing and social withdrawal do not change, and the social and relational aspects of the traumatic experience must be addressed.

Trauma and loss inevitably go hand in hand. Loss may be physical, psychological, relational, financial, and societal. Descent into mourning is both a necessary and dreaded task of this stage of recovery. Clients may resist mourning out of fear and out of pride. However, only through mourning everything one has lost (or missed due to the trauma) can one discover one's indestructible inner life. Sometimes people bypass mourning or outrage through fantasies of revenge, forgiveness or compensation. Yet, mourning is the only way to give due honor to loss. There is never adequate compensation, and neither hatred nor love can exorcise the trauma without appropriate mourning.

This stage in the process of transformation and liberation cannot be bypassed or hurried. The major work of the second stage is accomplished when the client reclaims his own history and feels renewed hope and energy to engage life. Time starts to move again. The client faces the task of rebuilding his life in the present moment and of pursuing aspirations for the future.

In the final stage of recovery from traumatic loss, the survivor faces the task of creating a future. After mourning the old self that the trauma destroyed, a person has to build a new self. She must develop new relationships to replace the loss of past relationships, which were tested and changed by her trauma. Old beliefs were challenged, and now a new sustaining faith must be found to replace them. In this stage, the survivor reclaims her world and life.

The first stage of recovery may be revisited as the survivor devotes energy to self-care as she engages the world and pursues old unfulfilled dreams or discovers aspirations for the first time. Empowerment and reconnection replace helplessness and isolation. During this stage, people may take controlled risks to challenge their fears. Physical challenges may be pursued, such as planned wilderness trips or self-defense training, to control fear and learn how to live with it and use it as a source of energy, enlightenment, and growth. Traditional male and female roles may be reevaluated and modified. Familial rules and roles may be challenged, as in breaking silence regarding alcohol, drug, sexual, or emotional abuses. The survivor must anticipate and plan for the possible outcomes, whatever they are.

The survivor re-creates a new self, both ideally and in actuality. Fantasy and imagination allow him to "try out" new freedoms and actions. This process reprograms thoughts, feelings, and behaviors. Life may become more ordinary, less dramatic, more peaceful. This is a "letting go" process of healing and forgiving oneself. Compassion and respect for the traumatized victim-self now join with celebrating the survivor-self. He feels pride in the qualities that helped him survive and courageously deal with the traumatic losses. He recognizes both his weaknesses and strengths, limitations and accomplishments, his self-care and connection to others and their assistance and support for the journey.

Appropriate trust is regained. The survivor feels autonomous and connected to others; she is able to maintain appropriate boundaries for herself and be respectful of others' boundaries; she takes greater initiative in her own life and is creating a new self-identity. She is ready and able to seek deeper, mutual relationships based on her true self. She is ready for greater intimacy.

★　★　★　★　★　★　★

Many people find resolution within their personal lives, apart from public view. However, there is a significant minority who, as a result of their trauma, use social action to transform the meaning of their personal tragedy into political or religious or social dimensions that serve mankind. The Make-a-Wish Foundation, for example, was co-created by the mother of a wonderful little boy who died with leukemia. The organization grants last wishes for over one hundred thousand children each year. Dr. Elisabeth Kubler-Ross used her German concentration camp experiences to advocate humane medical treatment of dying patients and help birth the hospice movement in America. MADD was born out of the loss of life from a drunk driver. Lisa Beamer became a spokesperson for 9/11 victims and created a foundation for the children without parents.

Social action becomes a source of power, using initiative, energy, and resourcefulness along with shared purpose, cooperation and alliance with others to achieve magnificent goals. This is coping behaviors at its highest form. It becomes a spiritual mission that transcends ordinary reality. These survivor missions raise public awareness and counteract the natural human response to horrific events, which is to put them out of mind. Their belief is that by speaking the unspeakable in public, they help others to be empowered and transformed. And in giving, they receive: healing, transformation, and the feeling of being loved, recognized and cared for themselves.

Resolution of trauma is never final or complete. At each stage of life, the impact potentially reverberates in new ways. The birth of a child, the death of a parent, the onset of old age, the empty nest syndrome, the loss of a job, the reaching a specific age oneself or seeing one's child reach a specific age, or great stress—all may trigger a relapse. The door back to support and renewal, if needed, should always remain ajar.

Psychologist Mary Harvey defines seven criteria for

trauma resolution: 1) physiological symptoms of post-traumatic stress disorder have become manageable; 2) the feelings associated with traumatic memories are bearable; 3) the person is in charge of his memories—he can remember or put them aside; 4) the traumatic memory is a coherent narrative and linked to feelings; 5) damaged self-esteem has been restored; 6) important relationships have been restored; 7) meaning and belief about the story have been reconstructed in a coherent system.

———————————

Destiny is not a matter of chance, it is a matter of choice; it is not a thing to be waited for, it is a thing to be achieved.

— William Jennings Bryan

Support Systems

Possibly the greatest resource we can have in life is our support systems. They increase our strength, effectiveness and confidence—and operate on the natural, spiritual law of synergism, "the simultaneous action of separate agencies which, together, have greater total effect than the sum of their individual effects." An uplifting, positive support system may be the single most powerful thing to help a person overcome fear and inertia and create change during crisis or loss.

Throughout the stories in this book, one of the threads that weaves through the coping process is the value of support systems. I include as "support systems" any person, group, organization—formal and informal—or relationship (with a person, with an animal, with God) which provides confidence, courage, and emotional and spiritual fortitude to overcome fears and move through life's challenges. If one looks in the paper, one can discover all kinds of support groups for many different situations, from business/sales/ professional organizations like BNI (Business Networking International), Kiwanis, or Toastmasters; to chronic illnesses and health problems, like AA or Al-Anon or fibromyalgia or grief support; to study groups, like those for books or religion or finances.

Groups like these meet together, share ideas and experiences, communicate insights they've learned, and encourage and reinforce each other. They meet a specific social, intellectual, financial, business, or emotional need. Some groups are open (anyone can join or attend); others are closed (only invited or committed persons participate, and the group is held privately). You can either join a group you may find that meets your needs, or you can create one yourself.

To form a support group, first decide on a focused purpose that you can communicate clearly to candidates for the group, such as dealing with loss, supporting each other as entrepreneurs, or personal or spiritual growth. Second, choose and qualify potential support group members. For intimate, long term sharing, I have found that single-gender groups work best. However, in groups where both male and females participate (such as divorce support groups), clearly established guidelines for interactions and relationships can be helpful. Consider whether potential members are trustworthy, positive, sharing and giving people who will benefit from participating in the group. Six to eight members is an ideal number for sharing in depth.

Meet with each of them for a visit to share the support system concept and explain how it will benefit them. Establish a first meeting time and place. Closed groups need a private setting where group members can communicate openly. Commit to a certain period of time, such as weekly or monthly, for six months or a year, etc. Establish any guidelines for the group, and in meetings always focus on your purpose. Leadership can be rotated/shared. Meetings should be positive, supportive, and confidential. Length of time for a meeting can be 1-2 hours.

Begin the group meeting by getting acquainted with each other and sharing why each chose to participate and what they expect from meetings. After the group is established, begin by making a "round" where each person can share something good that happened that week or a goal (even a tiny step) they achieved during week, and end by each person sharing something they gained in the meeting or what they want to do in the following week.

Group support can become an enormous tool for healing and bonding. In groups, people learn they are not alone or unique in human suffering. Therapeutic groups afford a degree of support and understanding that is not available in ordinary social environments. Feelings of isolation, shame, and stigma are dissolved as survivors hear the similar experiences of those who have endured similar ordeals. Groups develop cohesiveness and intimacy as individuals give and receive each other's gifts of tolerance, compassion, love, and mutually enhancing interaction. Self-esteem builds from group acceptance and mirroring painful feelings and self-disclosures. Members become more accepting as they experience acceptance and belonging, and integration of trauma occurs.

★ ★ ★ ★ ★ ★ ★

To be emotionally healthy, we need to give and receive love. We need both a vertical connection (with the Creator) and a horizontal connection (with fellow humans). We need to accept others and want the best to happen to them. We also have a basic need to have significant others in our lives who accept us and want the best to happen to us. There are four levels of relationships we need in order to function with optimal courage and minimal emotional clutter.

Level 1 - A very intimate, nonjudgmental relationship with at least one person with whom we can be totally open and feel totally accepted and acceptable. This relationship may be with a close friend or spouse, or with God. I personally believe one needs a relationship like this with God and at least another human being to stay grounded and grow. I also have observed that a pet may fill this void when a fellow human who gives nonjudgmental love and acceptance is missing. Pets provide stimulation and loving contact, as well as a non-judgmental, listening, supportive presence to humans.

Level 2 - An intimate, nonjudgmental relationship with a small group of people who foster giving and receiving unconditional support. It can be a support or study group. This can be with personal or career related friends or peers at work. It can also be you and your spouse and another couple. Like in Level 1 relationships, this one offers total acceptance of each other.

Level 3 - A friendly relationship with eight to twelve people, who are closely connected to you through church, work, business or civic groups and share common interests. This group has periodic meaningful interaction, though less intense or intimate. This is our closer social circles and friendships. These are often activity related.

Level 4 - A larger group wherein you receive less intense support or fellowship. These can be organizations, clubs, professional memberships, large churches, and civic groups like the Chamber of Commerce. These people are acquaintances and give enjoyment and the sense of belonging in a larger context. These relationships are loosely connected.

Our personalities, goals, and upbringing will determine how many relationships we have at each of these levels. Developing meaningful relationships takes emotional intelligence, which can be developed if one chooses. Loss and change in our lives change us as persons, and they can also change the nature of our relationships with others. When someone marries, divorces, or relocates, for example, relationships on all four levels must adjust to accommodate this external change.

When we go through changes in our lives, we need an adjustment period, a time to learn how to use our new wings of the heart. Be patient with yourself and with others. Our relationships with others will change as we grow and evolve. Some people support, applaud, or bless our wings; others fear, ignore, tolerate, or attack them. In the beautiful parable *Hope for the Flowers*, a caterpillar tells Yellow (who expresses fears about changing and other's reactions): "If you change, you can fly and show how beautiful butterflies are. Maybe (they) will want to become one, too." We need to love our wings, and give other people time, accept their resistance, listen to their fears, reassure them, share honestly with them, and quietly go on becoming our true divine self.

One of the great discoveries of life is that spiritual growth has no boundaries. As long as we like, there will be new wings to grow and larger life and soul aspects to emerge. Yes, even those of us who have known deep pain, losses, changes, and suffering, can fly! The Voice calls us to growth, to hope, to come to the edge, to spread our wings of courage—and gently pushes us into the wind of the spirit to help us lift our wings. Yes, there are bridges for coping. We can find our heart path to life and living again.

———————

Often people attempt to live their lives backward:
They try to HAVE more things or more money,
In order to DO more of what they want,
  so they will BE happier.
The way it actually works is the reverse.
You must first BE who you really are,
Then DO what you need to do,
In order to HAVE what you want.

— Margaret Young

PART THREE

RESOURCES

*There is something infinitely healing
in the repeated refrains of nature —
the assurance that dawn comes after night,
and spring after the winter.*

— Rachel Carson

Resources

Ever since my *A Ha!* introduction to psychologist Abraham Maslow and his Hierarchy of Needs crowned with self-actualization and peak experiences of spiritual growth during my junior year of college, I have actively pursued personal growth and development as a goal and avocation. It has been one of the most satisfying and pleasurable pursuits of my life, enriching others' and mine.

This Resource section includes a partial list of the information wealth available. Many of these are both alive for me and are on my personal shelves, read and reread. Some are mentioned in the text. Others were added because of my research for this book. Due to space limitations, other worthy sources are omitted. I hope you will enjoy these and use the list as an opportunity to begin your own exploration and discovery process and find comfort, healing, and new growth for your life journey. I offer them with gratitude to the authors for their wisdom and the ability to share them with you.

Attitudes and Perceptions Regarding Change

1. Change as Dealing With Anxiety

James Allen. *As a Man Thinketh.* Grosset and Dunlap, 1981.

Herbert Benson, M.D. *Beyond the Relaxation Response.* Times Books, 1984.

Joan Borysenko. *Guilt is the Teacher, Love is the Lesson.* Warner Books, 1990.

Rex Briggs, M.S.W. *Transforming Anxiety, Transcending Shame.* Health Communications, 1999.

Richard Carlson, Ph.D. *What About the BIG Stuff?* Hyperion, 2002. and *The Don't Sweat the Small Stuff Workbook.* Hyperion, 1998.

Deepak Chopra, M.D. *Unconditional Life: Discovering the Power to Fulfill Your Dreams.* Bantam, 1991.

Wayne W. Dyer. *There's a Spiritual Solution to Every Problem.* HarperCollins, 2001.

Eric Fromm. *The Art of Loving.* Bantam, 1956.

Daniel P. Goleman. *Emotional Intelligence.* Bantam, 1997.

Susan Jeffers, Ph.D. *Feel the Fear and Do It Anyway.* Fawcett, 1992.

Jon Kabat-Zinn. *Full Catastrophe Living: Using the Wisdom of Your Body and Mind to Face Stress, Pain and Illness.* Bantam Doubleday Dell, 1990.

Dr. Dharma Singh Khalsa, M.D. and Cameron Stauth. *Meditation as Medicine: Activate the Power of Your Natural Healing Force.* Fireside, 2001.

M. Scott Peck, M.D. *The Road Less Traveled.* Simon and Schuster, 1978.

Thom Rutledge. *Embracing Fear.* HarperCollins, 2002.

Hosea Silva. *The Silva Mind Control Method for Business Managers.* Pocket Books, 1983.

Post Traumatic Stress Disorder

Harriet B. Braiken, Ph.D. *The September 11 Syndrome.* McGraw-Hill, 2002.

Don R. Catherall, Ph.D. *Back From the Brink: A Family Guide to Overcoming Traumatic Stress.* Bantam, 1992.

Judith Lewis Herman, M.D. *Trauma and Recovery: The Aftermath of Violence, from Domestic Abuse to Political Terror.* Basic Books, 1997.

Aphrodite Matsakis, Ph.D. *Vietnam Wives: Facing the Challenges of Life with Veterans Suffering Post Traumatic Stress.* The Sidran Press, 1996.

www.ncptsd.org (PSTD information)

2. Change as Grief, Loss, and Mourning

William Bridges. *Transitions: Making Sense of Life's Changes.* Perseus Books, 1980. and *The Way of Transition: Embracing Life's Most Difficult Moments.* Perseus Publishing, 2001.

Eric Carle. *The Very Hungry Caterpillar.* (life cycle, ages 4-7). Philomon Books, 1987.

Nancy Cobb. *In Lieu of Flowers.* Pantheon, 2000.

Helen Fitzgerald. *The Mourning Handbook.* Simon and Schuster, 1994.

Jill Krementz. *How It Feels When a Parent Dies.* (ages 7-18, stories and photography). Knopf, 1988.

Doug Manning. Series of 4 Booklets: *Establishing Significance, Understanding Grief, The Gift of Understanding, Reconstructing Our Lives.* Insight Books, Inc., Drawer 2058, Hereford, Texas, 79045. (806) 364-7862.

Karen Moderow. *The Parting.* (funerals and memorial services). Jordan West Publications, 1996.

Mary C. Morrison. *Let Evening Come: Reflections on Aging.* Doubleday, 1998.

Sara E. Parrish. *How to Be a Parent for Your Parent.* Self-published, 2002. (order: 1-999-201-5811).

Catherine M. Sanders, Ph.D. *How to Survive the Loss of a Child.* Prima Publishing, 1992.

Mark H. Shearon. *Good Grief: Making Sense out of Death, Dying, and Funerals.* (order: www.bobproctor.com).

Judy Tatelbaum. *The Courage to Grieve.* Harper and Row, 1980.

E. B. White. *Charlotte's Web.* (ages 5-9). HarperTrophy, 1999.

Organizations

American Cancer Society, 1599 Clifton Road, Atlanta, GA 30329. (404) 320-3333. (212) 382-2169 (National Media Office).

The Compassionate Friends. P.O. Box 3696, Oak Brook, IL 60522-3696. (708) 990-0010.

National Hospice Organization. (800) 658-8898.

National Self-Help Clearinghouse, Room 620, Graduate School and University Center, City University of New York, 25 West 43rd Street, New York, NY 10036. (212) 642-2944.

Booklets

Karen Katafiasz. *Grief Therapy.* Abbey Press Publications. (Note: Abbey Press has about forty booklets on topics such as Prayer, Forgiveness, and Grief Therapy for Men in Self-Help booklets. To order call 1-800-325-2511. $4.95 each. Wonderful resource for adults and children.)

CD

Charlotte's Web 50th Anniversary CD Edition, Unabridged.
   2002 AudioBook.

Death and Dying

Mitch Albom. *Tuesdays With Morrie.* Doubleday, 1997.

Dr. Robert Buckman. *"I Don't Know What to Say..." How to
   Help and Support Someone Who is Dying.* Vintage Books,
   1992.

Maggie Callaman and Patricia Kelley. *Final Gifts.* Bantam,
   1992.

Forrest Carter. *The Education of Little Tree.* University of
   New Mexico Press, 1977.

Margaret Coberly, Ph.D., RN. *Sacred Passage.* Shambhala,
   2002.

Anita Diamant. *Saying Kaddish.* Schocken Books, 1988.

Joan Furman, M.S.N., RN, and David McNabb. *The Dying
   Time.* Bell Tower, Harmony Books, 1997.

Elizabeth Kubler-Ross, M.D. Death, *The Final Stage of
   Growth.* Prentice Hall, 1975.

— *On Death and Dying.* Touchstone, 1969.

— *The Tunnel and the Light.* Marlowe and Company, 1999.

— and David Kessler. *Life Lessons.* Simon and Schuster,
   2000.

Harriet Lerner. *The Dance of Anger.* HarperCollins, 1989.

Richard John Neuhaus. *As I Lay Dying.* Basic Books, 2002.

Henri J. M. Nouwen. *Our Greatest Gift.* HarperCollins, 1994.

Sherwin B. Nuland. *How We Die.* Vintage Books, 1993.

Mary Pipher, Ph.D. *Another Country.* Riverhead Books,
   1999.

Websites

www.atimetogrieve.net

www.griefandloss.org

www.aboutgoodgrief.com

www.bereavedfamilies.net/guide/index.html

www.dearheaven.com

www.dying.about.com

www.dreamseekercd.com (Downloadable Music; Note: CD is small letters.)

www.familygrief.com

www.geocities.com/Heartland/Falls/9648

www.angelfire.com/OK2/hope5/index.html

3. Change as Growth / Challenge

Julia Cameron. *The Artist's Way.* Putnam, 1992.

Stephen R. Covey. *The 7 Habits of Highly Effective People.* Simon and Schuster, 1989.

Shakti Gawain. *Creative Visualization.* Bantam, 1978.

Napoleon Hill. *Think and Grow Rich.* Fawcett Crest, 1960.

Gerald G. Jampolsky, M.D. *Love is Letting Go of Fear.* Bantam, 1970.

Lone Jensen. *Gifts of Grace.* HarperCollins, 1995.

Gloria D. Karpinski. *Where Two Worlds Touch.* Ballantine, 1990.

Richard J. Leider. *The Power of Purpose.* Fawcett Gold Medal, 1985.

Lawrence LeShan. *Cancer as a Turning Point.* Dutton, 1989.

Maxwell Maltz, M.D. *Psychocybernetics.* Pocket Books, 1960.

David McNally. *Even Eagles Need a Push.* TransForm Press, 1990.

M. Scott Peck, M.D. *The Road Less Traveled*. Simon and Schuster, 1978.

Rachel Naomi Remen. *Wounded Healers*. Wounded Healer Press, 1995.

Forrest C. Shaklee, Sr. *Thoughtsmanship*. Shaklee Corporation, 1994. (27th printing).

Denis Waitley. *Being the Best*. Pocket Books, 1987.

Audiocassette Tapes and Website

Larry Dossey, M.D. *The Power of Prayer: Connecting With the Power of the Universe*. Nightengale Conant. (1-800-572-2770). Website: www.nightengale.com

Earl Nightengale (audio and updates by Bob Proctor, protégée). *The New Lead the Field*. Nightengale Conant.

Support Systems for Change

Marriage and Family

Willard F. Harley, Jr., Ph.D. *His Needs, Her Needs.* Fleming H. Revell, 1986.

—. *I Cherish You.* Fleming H. Revell, 2002.

Susan Heither, Ph.D. *The Power of Two.* New Harbinger Publications, 1997.

Robert W. Herron, Ph.D. *Bridges to Intimacy: How to Make It through Midlife—with Your Spouse.* Thomas More Publishing, 2000.

Lois Kellerman and Nelly Bly. *Marriages from the Heart.* Viking Compass, 2002.

G. Frank Lawlis. *The Cure: The Hero's Journey with Cancer and The Caregiver's Guide to the Cure.* Resources Publications, 1994.

Jeanne Safer, Ph.D. *The Normal One: Life with a Difficult or Damaged Sibling.* The Free Press, 2002.

Virginia Satir. *The NEW Peoplemaking.* Science and Behavior Books, 1988.

Websites

www.marriagebuilders.com

www.somethingtoremembermeby.org

www.nightengale.com

Organizations

(See: **Change as Grief, Loss, and Mourning** section.)

Coping Behaviors for Change

Nature / Environment, Products

Rhoda Moyer Searcy's website: www.shaklee.net/rmsearcy.

Biodegradable cleaning products (benefit the earth and
    people sensitive to chemicals), water and air purifier,
    health, wellness, personal and skin care, nutrition and
    herbal products.
    www.shaklee.net/rmsearcy
    www.shaklee.com (Rhoda Searcy RE61105)
    www.greenmarketplace.com

First Climate Neutral Certified Company: Shaklee
    Corporation.

Creating backyard wildlife habitat and gardening seeds:
    www.eNature.com
    www.NationalWildlifeFederation.com
    www.Burpee.com (free online school to teach basics)
    www.Johnnyseeds.com (gift idea page)
    www.Tomatogrowers.com (tomatoes, peppers,
    tomatillos)

Nature Education:
    Timberlake Farm, 1501 Rock Creek Dairy Road,
    Whitsett, NC 27377. Phone: 336-449-0612;
    E-mail: TBLK1501@aol.com.

Prayer, Meditation, and Spirituality

Jim Castelli, ed. *How I Pray: People of Different Religions
    Share With Us That Most Sacred and Intimate Act of
    Faith.* Ballantine, 1994.

Larry Dossey, M.D. *Prayer is Good Medicine: How to Reap the Healing Benefits of Prayer.* HarperSan Francisco, 1996.

— *Reinventing Medicine: Beyond Mind-Body to a New Era of Healing.* HarperSan Francisco, 1999.

— *What We Can Do About the Unintentional Effects of Our Thoughts, Prayers, and Wishes.* HarperSan Francisco, 1998.

Chip Ingram. *I Am With You Always: Expressing God in Times of Need.* Baker Books, 2002.

James Kavanaugh. *God Lives: From Religious Guilt to Spiritual Freedom.* Steven J. Nash, 1993.

Naomi Levy. *Talking to God: Personal Prayers for Times of Joy, Sadness, Struggle, and Celebration.* Knopf, 1988.

— *To Begin Again.* Knopf, 1988.

Dale Matthews, David B. Larson, and Constance Barry. *The Faith Factor: An Annotated Bibliography of Clinical Research on Spiritual Subjects.* National Institute for Health Care Research, 6110 Executive Blvd., Suite 680, Rockville, MD 20952, 1995.

Elizabeth Roberts and Elios Amidon. *Life Prayers.* HarperSan Francisco, 1996.

— *Earth Prayers from Around the World.* HarperSan Francisco, 1991.

Bernie Siegel, M.D. *Prescriptions for Living: Inspirational Lessons for a Joyful, Loving Life.* HarperCollins, 1998.

Gabrielle Uhlein. *Meditations with Hildegard of Bingen.* Bear, 1983.

Dr. Bruce H. Wilkinson. *The Prayer of Jabez.* Multnomah Publishers, 2002.

Hope and Inspiration Websites and Crisis Services

www.crystalcathedral.org

www.hourofpower.org

www.newhopeonline.org (hotline for crises)

www.newteen.org (hotline for teens)

Organizations and Publications

Creation: Earthy Spirituality. Published by Matthew Fox's
organization. A spiritually optimistic, celebratory
theology that integrates theology, science, and
psychology. Write to Subscription Department,
Creation Magazine, 160 Virginia Street, #290,
San Jose, California, 95112.

Living Enrichment Center. 29500 S.W. Grahams Ferry
Road, Wilsonville, Oregon, 97070. 1-800-893-1000.
Offers free catalogue of inspirational books and tapes
by Mary Manin Morrissey and other spiritual teachers.

The Simonton Cancer Center. P.O. Box 890, Pacific
Palisaides, CA, 90272. (310) 459-4434.

The Spindrift Foundation. A nondenominational Christian
group that does highly rigorous research on prayer.
Often very technical. Available to public. Write to
Spindrift, Inc., P.O. Box 5134, Salem, Oregon,
97304-5134.

Yoga Journal. Covers a broad range of healing. Write to
Yoga Journal, P.O. Box 3755, Escondido, CA, 92033.

Music

Patrick Bernhart. *Atlantis Angelis.*

Clannad. *The Magical Ring.*

A Feather on the Breath of God. Gregorian chant-like, of
12th century Christian mystic Hildegard of Bingen.

Robbie Gass and On Wings of Song. *Many Blessings*. (long chants, includes Om Namah Shivaya)

Osami Kitajima. *The Source*.

Daniel Kobialka, classical violinist. *Timeless Motion* (includes Pachebel's "Canon").

—. *Path of Joy*. (includes "Jesu, Joy of Man's Desiring").

Ray Lynch. *Deep Breakfast*.

Thérèse Schroeder-Sheker. *Rosa Mystica*.

Movies

City of Joy. An American doctor loses a patient and goes to India to find himself.

The Son's Room. A portrait of a closely knit Italian family whose contented middle class existence is shattered with the death of the teenage son, Andrea, in a scuba-diving accident. Winner of the Palme D' Or at the Cannes International Film Festival.

Rituals, Touch, and Music

Pat B. Allen. *Art is a Way of Knowing: A Guide to Self-knowledge and Spiritual Fulfillment through Creativity*. Boston: Shambhala, 1995.

Sedonia Cahill and Joshua Halpern. *Ceremonial Circle*. HarperSan Francisco, 1992.

Don Campbell. *Music and Miracles*. Quest, 1992.

—, ed. *Music, Physician for Times to Come*. Quest, 1992.

Barbara Dossey, Lynn Keegan, Cathie E. Guzzetta, and Leslie Kalkmeier. *Holistic Nursing: A Handbook for Practice*. Aspen, 1995.

Noreen Cavan Frisch and Jane Kelley. *Healing Life's Crises: A Guide for Nurses*. Delmar, 1996.

Dorothea Hover-Kramer. *Healing Touch: A Resouce for Health Care Professionals.* Delmar, 1996.

Delores Krieger. *Accepting Your Power to Heal.* Bear, 1993.

Stanley Krippner and Patricia Welch. *Spiritual Dimensions of Healing.* Irvington, 1992.

Belleruth Naparstek. *Staying Well with Guilded Imagery.* Warner, 1994.

Ilana Rubenfeld. *The Listening Hand.* Bantam Books, 2000.

Jean Sayre-Adams and Steve Wright. *The Theory and Practice of Therapeutic Touch.* Churchill Livingstone, 1995.

O. Carl Simonton and Reid Henson. *The Healing Journey.* Bantam, 1994.

Audio-Visual and Journal Resources

Dr. Frank A. Corbo, D.C., Senior Editor. *Chiropractic Wellness and Fitness Magazine.* Issue One, 2002. CW & FM, 1330 E. Katella Avenue, Anaheim, CA 92805. 1-800-640-1089.

Barbara M. Dossey, Lynn Keegan, and Cathie E Guzzetta. *The Art of Caring.* (4 audiocassette tape series). Sounds True Audio, 1996. 800-333-9185.

Dr. Larry Dossey, M.D., Exec. Ed. *Alternative Therapies in Health and Medicine.* Alternative Therapies, P.O. Box 611, Holmes, PA 19043. 1-800-345-8112.

Janet F. Quinn. *Therapeutic Touch: A Home Study Video Course for Family Caregivers.* National League for Nursing, 1996. Phone: 1-800-669-9656 ext. 138.

Exercise, Health, and Wellness

Wellness care encompasses overall health and well-being: physical, emotional, mental, spiritual, social, and financial, including career and lifestyle choices. This section will include a sampling of resources supporting optimal health and well-being as a whole person.

Books: Physical

Dr. Paula Baille-Hamilton, M.D., Ph.D. *The Detox Diet.* Michael Joseph, 2002.

James F. Balch, M.D. and Phyllis A. Balch, C.N.C. *Prescription for Nutritional Healing.* Avery Publishing Group, 1990.

Dr. Bruce Miller, Certified Nutrition Specialist. *The Nutrition Guarantee.* The Summit Publishing Group, 1998.

Physicians Guide to Nutriceuticals. Nutritional Data Resources, L.P., 1998 Charter Edition. www.PGN-NDR.com; 1-888-288-7920.

Prevention's Healing With Vitamins. Rodale Press, 1996.

Linda J. Prosak. *Take the Road to Health.* Linda J. Prosak, 2002. website: www.ilovedieting.com. User name: Diet; Password: Diet.

Miriam E. Nelson, Ph.D. *Strong Women Stay Young.* Bantam, 1997.

Christiane Northrup, M.D. *Women's Bodies, Women's Wisdom.* Bantam, 1994.

Gary Yanker. *Walk-Shaping.* Hearst Books, 1995.

Yoga: Mind and Body. Sivananda Yoga Vedanta Center, DK Publishing, 1996.

Books: Emotional, Mental, Spiritual

Joan Wester Anderson. *Where Angels Walk.* Ballantine, 1992.

Deepak Chopra. *Journey Into Healing: Awakening the Wisdom Within You.* Harmony Books, 1994.

—. and David Simon. *Grow Younger, Live Longer. 10 Steps to Reverse Aging.* Harmony Books, 2001.

Kenneth S. Cohen. *Strong as the Mountain, Supple as Water: The Way of Qigong.* Ballantine, 1996.

Norman Cousins. *Anatomy of an Illness.* Norton, 1979.

—. *Head First: The Biology of Hope.* Dutton, 1989.

Daniel Goleman and Joel Gurin, eds. *Mind-Body Medicine: How to Use Your Mind for Better Health.* Consumer Reports Books, 1993.

Blair Justus, Ph.D. *Who Gets Sick: Thinking and Health.* Peak Press, 1987.

Rita Justus, Ph.D. *Alive and Well.* Peak Press, 1995.

Sue Monk Kidd. *When the Heart Waits.* HarperSan Francisco, 1990.

Vashtie M. McKenzie. *Journey to the Well.* Viking Compass, 2002.

Mary Manin Morrissey. *Building Your Field of Dreams.* Bantam, 1996.

Frances Vaughn. *The Inward Arc: Healing in Psychotherapy and Spirituality.* Blue Dolphin, 1995.

Websites on Wellness / Living Foods

www.gardenofhealth.com

www.living-foods.com

www.quintessencerestaurant.com

www.rawfood.com

www.sunfood.com

www.tanglewoodwellnesscenter.com

Jobs / Careers / Business / Financial

Robert G. Allen. *Multiple Streams of Income.* John Wiley and Sons, 2000.

— and Mark Victor Hanson. *The One Minute Millionaire.* Harmony Books, 2002.

—. *The Road to Wealth.* Simon and Schuster, 1987.

The Business School for People Who Like Helping People: The Eight Hidden Values of a Network Marketing Business, Other than Making Money. Tech Press, Inc., 2001.

Martha I. Finney. *In the Face of Uncertainty: 25 Top Leaders Speak Out on Challenge, Change, and the Future of American Business.* Amacom, 2002.

Michael Gerber. *The E-Myth Revised.* Harper Collins Publishers, 2001.

Robert T. Kiyosaki. *The Cashflow Quadrant.* Warner Books, 1999.

—. *Rich Dad, Poor Dad.* Warner Books, 1997.

—. *Rich Dad's Prophecy.* Warner Books, 2002.

Networking Times: Moving the Heart of Business. Bob Proctor, for Gabriel Media Group, Inc. 2002. Monthly magazine. Subscribe online at www.networkingtimes.com or call 866-343-4005.

Paul Zane Pilzer. *The Wellness Revolution.* Wiley, 2002.

Bob Proctor. *You Were Born Rich.* Life Success Productions, 1997.

Wallace D. Wattles. *The Science of Getting Rich.* Life Success Productions, 1996.

Websites

www.bobproctor.com

www.multiplestreamsofincome.com

www.rhodaseary.com

www.robertallen.com

www.thewellnessrevolution.info

Important Questions for Couples to Discuss and Share to Avoid "Nasty Surprises" about Finances:

1. What are our financial plans for retirement?

2. What are my financial options and resources if my spouse died?

3. What and where are the documents and other crucial information I'll need?

4. Are my documents such as Living Will and Will current?

Information on Story Contributors

Damien Birkel. See his story, pages 72-73.

Sue Erdmann. Lupus expert. (920) 262-7455. 827 Richards Avenue, Waterton, Wisconsin, 53094. Email: erverd@charter.net.

Dr. Nancy O'Reilly. Clinical Psychologist and Consultant who does research on women and aging. www.womenspeak.com site includes very helpful information on stress management and coping, as well as seminars she offers.

Beula Peele. MSW Social Worker and Consultant for health care agencies on the needs of geriatric clients; Support Group facilitator. Contact information: 543 Rosemont Drive, Broadway, VA, 22815.

Cover Art

Steven W. Dunn, the artist, is a native of North Carolina and produces artwork for clients throughout the eastern U.S. Dunn says that with "Heart Path"© he wants to convey a sense of hope and contentment as we move from one stage of life on to a new and brighter phase.

The art is available as a signed giclée reproduction. Paper size: 8 x 11 inches; image size: 5 x 8 inches; reproduced on archival-quality paper.

- -

I would like to order _____ (number) "Heart Path" ©
signed giclée reproductions by Steven W. Dunn.

"Heart Path" © by Steven W. Dunn $50.00 ea. . . $ _____

6% sales tax (NC residents only) $3.25 ea. ...... $ _____

Postage and packaging $15.00 ea. .... $ _____

TOTAL .... $ _____

Name _____

Address _____

City/State/Zip _____

Phone Number (Daytime) _____

Authorized Signature _____

Make check or money order payable to: **Steven W. Dunn**. Please allow four to six weeks for delivery.

Mail to: Rooster Ridge Studio, 2944 Fraternity Church Road, Winston-Salem, NC 27127-8774. Phone: (336) 650-9180.